Theatre and nationalism

in twentieth-century Ireland

Theatre and nationalism in twentieth-century Ireland

EDITED BY ROBERT O'DRISCOLL

University of Toronto Press

1971

© University of Toronto Press 1971
Toronto and Buffalo
Printed in Great Britain for University of Toronto Press
Reprinted 1973
ISBN 0–8020–1700–2
LC 77–15183

Frontispiece
What stood in the Post Office/With Pearse and Connolly?
Richard Murphet as Cuchulain

Contents

Illustrations

Contributors

DAVID R. CLARK
Professor of English, University of Massachusetts

GEORGE MILLS HARPER
University Professor and Dean of Arts and Science,
Virginia Polytechnic Institute

DAVID KRAUSE
Professor of English, Brown University

THOMAS MacANNA
Artistic Director in the Abbey Theatre, Dublin

ROGER MCHUGH
Professor of Anglo-Irish Literature, University College, Dublin

ROBERT O'DRISCOLL
Associate Professor of English, St. Michael's College,
University of Toronto

ANN SADDLEMYER
Professor of English, University of Victoria

MICHAEL J. SIDNELL
Associate Professor of English, Trinity College, University of Toronto

FRANCIS WARNER
Fellow of St Peter's College, Oxford

Introduction

ROBERT O'DRISCOLL

A national literature, Yeats writes, 'is the work of writers who are moulded by influences that are moulding their country, and who write out of so deep a life that they are accepted there in the end.'[1] 'This race and this country and this life produced me,' James Joyce writes in *A Portrait of the Artist as a Young Man*, 'I shall express myself as I am.'[2] For Yeats and Joyce an artist's soul comes first, not his country; by expressing that soul as it was, the artist, they felt, was inevitably expressing the deeper thoughts and desires of his race.

This book is about the writers who have moulded the mind of modern Ireland. Initially they upset their countrymen's preconceptions and propaganda, for they presented Ireland, not as her political apologists would wish her to be seen, but as she was. They turned from the fashionable and narrowly nationalistic, and wrote not from observation but from personal experience, presenting in their work their own passionate personalities, creating from the shock of new material a unique style, the opposite of what their nation demanded or expected. Like the Greeks and the Elizabethans, they were gifted with a sensitive dangerous audience, an audience reluctant to relinquish its grasp on familiar form and thought.

The fact that Dublin was a small homogeneous city increased the tension between artist and audience. As well as being a name on a theatre programme, the dramatist was a personal presence. Religious, political, and folk traditions had trained the people to listen, but they had not yet lost the sense of individual importance essential to the evaluation of what they heard and saw. The artist presented on the stage a vision that shattered complacent attitudes and abstractions, but the audience, acutely sensitive to the image of their country presented publicly, felt called upon to do battle for what it believed to be the honour of the nation.

Two events, one literary and one historical, lie behind the development of a cultural nationalism in nineteenth-century Ireland. The literary event was the publication in the early 1760s of James Macpherson's translations of what he claimed were authentic poems of Ossian. These, as every undergraduate knows, were forgeries in that they purported to be translations of a third-century poet; nevertheless, they did have a profound influence on European literature and attracted attention to a body of tradition which to that point had only been locally known. Societies were formed to examine and publish the manuscripts in which the Irish tradition was preserved,[3] and a number of independent scholars attempted to prove their country's claim to an ancient and honourable literature and history.[4]

The other event that lies behind the development of a cultural nationalism during nineteenth-century Ireland, the historical event, was the founding in 1791 of the United Irish Society, which proposed as its chief object the abolition of 'all unnatural religious distinctions,' the union of Irishmen 'against the unjust influence of Great Britain,' and the establishment of 'true representation in a national Parliament.'[5] It was broken as a political force in 1798, but in 1810 its principles were altered from a political to an educational ideal, as the writer of the original prospectus of the Society, William Drennan, founded the Royal Belfast Academical Institution, setting down as one of its chief aims (and this is significant when we remember that this was before Catholic emancipation) the encouragement of communication between 'pupils of all religious denominations ... by frequent and friendly intercourse, in the common business of education, by which means a new turn might be given to the national character and habits, and all the children of Ireland should know and love each other.'[6] From an educational to a literary ideal is, in the hindsight of history, a natural transition : it was attempted by one of the pupils of the Academical Institution, Samuel Ferguson, who advocated that a national literature would not only be the means of realising the cultural destiny which he considered rightfully Ireland's, but would also provide a link between people of diverse convictions : it would minimise and ultimately remove the antipathies between Orange and Green, Protestant and Catholic, aristocrat and peasant. To this end he dedicated a long life of versatile literary activity. He turned from the conventional poetic themes of his day to ancient Irish history and legend. He dignified and popularised this material and made it the subject matter of a new and distinctive literature.

In the perspective of literary history Ferguson is the seminal figure in nineteenth-century Anglo-Irish literature. In his paper on 'Intellectual Nationalism' and 'Intellectual Hatred,' however, George Harper traces the birth of cultural nationalism to Thomas Davis, and to some extent he is right, for it was Davis who popularised in *The Nation,* during the 1840s, the ideas that Ferguson had first articulated in the *Dublin University Magazine* during the eighteenthirties. What Yeats calls 'intellectual nationalism,' then, has its beginnings in Ferguson and – although Yeats never approved of the Young Ireland subjection of literature to politics – to some extent in Davis. The opposite principle, 'intellectual hatred,' that of blind hatred of England and blind love of a nationalistic abstraction, the principle that subsequently fed the revolutionaries and secret societies, can be traced to John Mitchel. Both movements, cultural nationalism and intellectual hatred, come to culmination in the early part of the twentieth century, but, as Professor Harper perceptively observes, the great art that came as a consequence of the one may not have been possible without the 'abrasive stimulant' of the other :

Even the wisest man grows tense
With some sort of violence
Before he can accomplish fate,
Know his work or choose his mate.[7]

Great moments of theatrical achievement have often coincided with moments of national excitement and tension. In times of acute national consciousness the theatre is the form of literature which makes the most direct impact on the people, becoming at times a means for propaganda, but ultimately the means by which the deeper life of the people is expressed. For the theatre in art is the equivalent of the market-place in life, and in late nineteenth-century Dublin the market-place had not yet been forgotten by the people. At the point of renaissance, a meeting-point of the mythic and the scientific, the tribal and the commercial, a point when the past is re-evaluated and rediscovered in the light of changing values and iconoclastic discoveries, something vital and new is created. Myth and legend assume sudden significance; the antiquary and historian attempt to trace the cultural and historical beginnings of the nation, and the artist, by consciously choosing for subject the life and legends of the people, by restoring to topographical sites their former heroic associations and by giving them new levels of poetic association, is inspired by an ideal similar to that which inspires the politician.

After the death of Parnell in 1891, David Krause argues, cultural and political nationalism had an urgent need of each other's vitality and vision, as both worked towards the common goal of liberating Ireland from British political and literary domination. Indeed, after the fall of Parnell, when national independence seemed impossible, much of the energy that had been sunk in Irish politics was diverted to literature. But the political and cultural nationalists were destined to part company when the reality of an independent state seemed imminent. For at that point, as Yeats pointed out, the political nationalist became enchanted by the abstraction of his own ideals:

Hearts with one purpose alone
Through summer and winter seem
Enchanted to a stone
To trouble the living stream.[8]

For the artist there is only the living stream and the truth he discovers in his ever-changing heart.

Nineteenth-century Irish theatre had been chiefly melodramatic, a conflict of good against evil, of victim against villain, of rebel against oppressor. Complications were carefully contrived and arbitrarily resolved, and it is understandable that in a time of political, social, and artistic deprivation a nation should present on the stage life as it would want it to be rather than life as it was. The Irish Literary Theatre, which was founded in 1899 by Yeats, Lady Gregory, and Edward Martyn, broke dramatically with the political and melodramatic traditions:

We propose to have performed in Dublin, in the spring of every year certain Celtic and Irish plays, which whatever be their degree of excellence will be written with a high ambition, and so to build up a Celtic and Irish school of dramatic literature. We hope to find in Ireland an uncorrupted and imaginative audience trained to listen by its passion for oratory, and believe that our desire to bring upon the stage the deeper thoughts and emotions of Ireland will ensure for us a tolerant welcome, and that freedom to experiment which is not found in theatres of England, and without which no new movement in art or literature can succeed. We will show that Ireland is not the home of buffoonery and of easy sentiment, as it has been represented, but the home of an ancient idealism. We are confident of the support of all Irish people, who are weary of misrepresentation, in carrying out a work that is outside the political questions that divide us.[9]

Nineteenth-century Anglo-Irish literature had not the confidence to confront the truth, and it was, perhaps, only with the imminence of independence that writers could begin to face the truth about their country and themselves.

In 1909 Synge proclaimed that before poetry could 'be human again it must learn to be brutal.'[10] In their plays Synge and O'Casey present with uncompromising brutality the suffering of people who in the deprivations of their daily lives found little solace in nationalistic abstractions, whose only weapons for survival were not 'fabricated' idealisms but their own native cunning and their own native imagination and wit. Yeats and Joyce defended the artist's right to present the bitter unwelcome truth; and Synge and O'Casey 'instinctively adopted this idea as an implicit principle' and without explanation went on to flatten the unsubstantiated idealisms of the nationalists. As a consequence, they were 'more violently controversial figures' in the Ireland of their time than even Yeats and Joyce, and the 'self-appointed guardians' of the national honour, suspicious from the start of the motives and methods of the Abbey dramatists, and sensitive to the image of Ireland presented at home and abroad, were inflamed by the picture of the Irish peasant Synge presented in his plays: 'Synge found the Irish peasants in varying states of comic paralysis and contradictory tensions, straining under the complex moods of frustration and wild fantasy, vicarious exuberance and farcical despair, and therefore his dark comedies were a necessary desecration of those sentimental pieties of the idyllic and pure peasant life.'[11]

In the case of O'Casey the reaction was more violent, and even today some of his countrymen have not forgiven him. Yet in his early brutal plays, where the women heroically face the realities of daily life, while their men are lost in illusions, sustained by nationalism, alcohol, and poetry, O'Casey is in some ways merely extending the range of Cathleen, focusing not on the ethereal traditional queen of Pearse and Yeats, but on the other Cathleen, 'coarsely dressed, hair a little tousled ... barefooted, sometimes with a whiff of whiskey off her breath; brave and brawny; at ease in the smell of sweat and the sound of bad language, vital, and asurge with immortality.'[12] To identify Cathleen ni Houlihan with the 'ragged women of the Dublin tenements'; to make the 'scapegoats of the slums' his main concern instead of the patriots at the barricades; to suggest that the fight for national independence could bring out the worst as well as the best in men; to hint that the 'heroes' themselves had fear hidden in their hearts and human longings to return to the women and unborn children they were torn from for an illusion – all this was, David Krause argues, a 'desecration of Ireland's household gods.' But this 'desecration,' this mockery of national ideals, was necessary before the nation could be fully mature: 'perhaps a nation needs the comic wisdom of its irreverent fools as well as the martyred blood of its patriots; perhaps Ireland was not ready for her freedom until her conception of herself was broad enough for the national character to encompass a Fluther Good as well as a Patrick Pearse.'[13] Roger McHugh's evocation of the tragedy and humour of the Rising is a mark of the maturity of the nation.

All theatrical and all nationalistic endeavours begin and end in the casual comedy of our daily lives. Indeed, Yeats's conception of the symbolic theatre is closely related to the conception of nationalism he evolved during his career. The symbolic dramatist, he argued, seeks through the interrelation of the arts, through verse, movement, music, song, and dance, to present on the stage the opposite of all that we are in everyday life, a noble unified image that begins and ends in the absurdity of material life. With ancient legend for subject the poetic dramatist could attain the distance from life that makes credible strange events, elaborate words, and could excite in one visionary but vulnerable moment the mystery and innocence that existed before man fell a slave to the external world.

Similarly, in a moment of political revolution, people forget for a time their daily concerns. Indeed, F. X. Martin maintains that the 1916 Rising was consciously staged as a drama: Pearse, Plunkett, and MacDonagh were poets and playwrights, and the theatrical element was conspicuous in the dress and public gestures of some of the other leaders:

The leaders of the revolt saw themselves as inheritors of Ireland's tragic past, committed willy-nilly to violent action in order to arrest the attention of their complacent countrymen, but playing in fact for the benefit and applause of future generations of Irishmen. However unreal the play may have seemed beforehand, however disturbing the uncertainty which at times may have chilled the hearts of the more reflective of the conspirators during the months of preparation, there is no doubt that Pearse and his companions showed an unerring theatrical instinct in the *mise en scène,* in the roles they chose and the lines they spoke.

As a centre-piece for the drama the General Post Office was selected; it was a disastrous choice as a military headquarters but since it stood prominently on one side of the main thoroughfare of the city its seizure meant that not only would all normal activity in Dublin be disrupted but from it defiance would be trumpted for everyone to hear. The classical front of the G.P.O., with its Ionic pillars and portico, was to serve as an admirable background for Pearse reading the proclamation, as it was to be an awe-inspiring sight on Friday night, its pillars and roof wrapped in tongues of flame, amid the swelling orchestration of rifle-fire, machine-gun chatter, bursting hand-grenades and booming artillery, presenting a Wagnerian grand finale to Easter Week. ... The dramatic incidents were vivid not because they had the terrifying character of huge armies, impersonal, implacable, and bloody – as were at this time darkening the landscape in northern France and Belgium – but because they laid bare the heroic qualities of individual men and women ... [14]

But the spiritual image that the revolutionary or the symbolic dramatist presents must begin and end in the absurdity of daily life, and after the play or revolution the participants must return to the absurd world from which the image blossomed. In Yeats's *The Death of Cuchulain,* for example, the two central characters of the play,

Cuchulain and the Blind Man, seem to embody the heroism and absurdity that is implicit in all theatre and in all nationalism. A spiritual image may be created, but the image, like man, is as vulnerable as visionary :

What stood in the Post Office
With Pearse and Connolly?

'The heroic and the absurd,' we may answer. There is indeed an implicit absurdity in all heroic action. For the things that men adore and loathe are, as Yeats indicates at the end of *The Death of Cuchulain*, perhaps the same, and this is the bitter knowledge that both the symbolic dramatist and the nationalist must discover.

Two Irish dramatists, George Bernard Shaw and Samuel Beckett, stood outside the problems that confronted their contemporary dramatists in Ireland. Nationalism to Shaw was an aggressive 'mode of self-consciousness,'[15] an 'agonising symptom of a suppressed natural function,' a necessary but retrograde step that stood between Ireland and the light of the world.[16] For Shaw the ideal political arrangement was a federation of nationalities, but before a healthy British federation could be established Ireland had first to be given control of her own affairs. A federation, Shaw argues, is the third and final step in man's political progress : the individual must first secure his personal liberty and then his national liberty; he must enlarge 'his social consciousness from his individual self to the nation of which he is a unit,' and this instinct for personal and national liberty is 'as a burning fire in his bones.'[17]

Nationalities must first be realised before they can be federated, Shaw snaps in 1888.[18] But Ireland, having achieved its national independence, should realise that national independence is impossible. The world, Shaw remarks, will not work 'in nation-tight compartments' and nations must establish as much 'organic connection' with each other as is compatible with their own individuality.[19] We are

'Europeans and citizens of the world,'[20] Shaw protests at the age of ninety, and, either Ireland must integrate itself with the British and European community, or else must become a Robinson Crusoe island and slip back into the Atlantic as a 'little green patch.'[21]

Throughout his life Shaw's chief concern was with the wider British federation, and he used his Irish nationality whenever it was to his advantage to do so, as a switch to beat John Bull. His destiny, he felt, was 'to educate London,'[22] to argue, amuse, and bully 'the English out of their follies.'[23] Like Edmund Burke, he believed his class to be the true guardians of the British heritage and he himself the self-appointed conscience of the British nation.

Samuel Beckett takes us beyond nationalism, and it may be that nationalism in either a political or cultural sense is now outdated and outstated. Nationalism to Beckett means roots. Roots are nurtured by memory and habit, and while these qualities may make daily life bearable, the artist must defy the arbitrary order of both. Beckett's novels present the dilemma of characters who in their eccentricity have not yielded to these secure controls, characters who possess what Proust calls 'involuntary memory' and which was for Beckett the source of all artistic apprehension. Once this artistic apprehension takes place, however, its articulation must assume an order similar to that which it has to defy in the first place. The artist, therefore, must consciously cultivate failure, and it is this failure that Beckett attempts to present in his novels. But in this design a fundamental tension is created between the characters in the work and the artist behind the work, because behind the tedium and disintegration of the creative attempts of the characters there is the controlling mind of Samuel Beckett. That is why, when Beckett focuses only on the unartistic world in the plays, his art is more happy: 'His art is happy, but who knows his mind?'[24]

Beckett's plays do not have the definite settings that the cultural nationalist would want, but still the characters in the plays are sustained by the memory and habit that sustain rooted men. His inditement of modern man, therefore, is as applicable to the internationalist as it is to the nationalist.

The papers published in this book were read at the second inter-university Seminar in Irish Studies, held at St Michael's College, University of Toronto, between 28 November and 1 December 1968. The Irish Studies Seminar Committee (Robert O'Driscoll, W. J. Keith, George Falle, Michael Sidnell, and Eric Domville) and its Advisory Committee (Douglas LePan, M. H. M. MacKinnon, and Desmond Pacey) is deeply grateful to the following for financial assistance to the conference: the Canada Council, St Michael's College, University of Toronto School of Graduate Studies, Ontario Department of Education (Educational and Cultural Exchange Program), Graduate Centre for the Study of the Drama (University of Toronto), Irish International Airlines, The Macmillan Company of Canada, and The Irish Tourist Board.

In addition to the papers read during the seminar, we also presented with the help of the Centre for the Study of Drama and under the direction of Thomas MacAnna a sound and light history of the Abbey Theatre and a production of Yeats's *The Death of Cuchulain*. The reception the play received suggests that maybe at last a need for the ritualistic type of play that Yeats wrote is beginning to be expressed.

We are deeply grateful to Senator Michael Yeats for permission to quote from his father's published works, for permission to publish the seven letters from his father to George Bernard Shaw, and especially for the lectures of Yeats that are published in this book. The copyright of this material remains with Senator Yeats. We are also grateful to the following for permission to quote from published works: Macmillan & Co. Ltd. for quotations from W. B. Yeats, Sean O'Casey, and Frank O'Connor; the Public Trustee and the Society of Authors for quotations from Shaw; the Society of Authors as the literary representative of the estate of James Joyce and The Viking Press, Inc. for quotations from Joyce's *A Portrait of the Artist as a Young Man* and 'The Day of the Rabblement'; Macmillan & Co. Ltd. for quotations from Yeats, from O'Connor's *An Only Child,* and from O'Casey's *The Shadow of the Gunman, Juno and the Paycock,* and *The Plough and the Stars*; Alfred A. Knopf, Inc. for permission to quote from O'Connor's *An Only Child,* © Alfred A. Knopf, Inc.; Faber and Faber Ltd., Grove Press, Inc., and Calder and Boyars for quotations from Beckett's *Endgame, Play, Krapp's Last Tape, Waiting for Godot, Happy Days, All That Fall,* and *Come and Go*; Rupert Hart-Davis for quotations from *The Letters of W. B. Yeats*; Rupert Hart-Davis and Atlantic-Little, Brown and Co. for the quotation from Sean O'Faolain's *Vive Moi*; Victor Gollancz Ltd. for quotations from Maud Gonne's *A Servant of the Queen.*

To my friends, Lorna Reynolds and Ian Fletcher, I am indebted for suggestions for the introduction.

Stars of the Abbey's ascendancy

ANN SADDLEMYER

'They do be putting quare plays on in Dublin nowadays! ... Very quare plays. They do be putting on plays where a boy from the country kills his da!'
'That seems wrong.'
'Yes. And they make us out to be nothing but cutthroats, and murderers, and dijinerates.'
'What on earth do they mean by doing that?'
'They calls it – ART.'[1]

'If we all told the story we would all tell it differently,' Yeats commented towards the end of his life of his perilous career as master of that Irish *Patna*, the Abbey Theatre. Thirty years and at least three hundred more versions of the story have been added since 1937, all with the infinite variety resulting from an irresistible temptation to cap one Irishman's story with a better one – on the same subject. Actors, authors, audiences have recreated the early days of Ireland's National Theatre, adding, subtracting, muting, or intensifying the strange collaboration of national and literary characteristics that, while making such a unique movement possible in the first place, made the chances of its continued success forever implausible.

Some facts we do know; they are established by the diligent reporting of national newspapers and that other monument to Ireland's life and times, Joseph Holloway. We have playbills, photographs, directors' memoranda, the occasional rejection slip, to confirm them. Above all, there is the Abbey Theatre itself, not the original building nor – except on rare historic occasions – the original plays. But a company of players exists, and an audience attends them. 'Actors may come, actors may go,' remarked the prosaic Holloway, 'and dramatists and patrons do likewise, but the dramatic movement goes on.'[2] We will leave a cautious chronological outline of the facts for the moment, then, and, peering round both sides of the curtain, briefly explore some of the forces – or, if you like, ideals – which made that dramatic movement possible and determined its course. 'They calls it – ART.'

Certainly in retrospect art contributed a great deal to the phenomenon we have come to call the Abbey Theatre movement: (W. B. Yeats, 'The Municipal Gallery Revisited')

> John Synge, I and Augusta Gregory, thought
> All that we did, all that we said or sang
> Must come from contact with the soil, from that
> Contact everything Antaeus-like grew strong.
> We three alone in modern times had brought
> Everything down to that sole test again,
> Dream of the noble and the beggar-man.

Many would question the arrogant exclusion of players and philanthropists who made that song possible – the Fay brothers, Edward Martyn, and Annie Horniman to name only four – but no one can deny that the history and fame of the Irish Theatre are inextricably bound up with this powerful triumvirate, 'John Synge, I and Augusta Gregory.' Very early their own plays surpassed the limitations of players and audience, but while even one remained at the helm the power remained firmly in their hands, and the principles established

were by their will. In fact, Synge's presence became even more marked
after his death. In 1915, Yeats could dismiss players' and manager's
complaints with the statement, 'Synge has left us a glorious heritage,
and I have worked to make the theatre a Synge theatre.'³ In 1928, at
the age of 76, Lady Gregory records in her diary a hard day's revision
of another play – by a new playwright. And Yeats himself, although
despairing many years earlier of finding on this stage his own Temple
of Drama, controlled, albeit remotely, the policies and affairs of the
Abbey Theatre until his death.

It is difficult to say precisely when the movement began, or which
of the many contributing forces first made itself felt. Yeats had been
writing plays ever since boyhood; Synge had begun his first play – in
German – long before he had even heard of his own country's upsurge
of nationalism and with far too little playgoing experience; Lady
Gregory, during her social days as wife to the urbane Sir William, had
never particularly cared for the plays of the London season. All three
first met in 1896, but here again it is only retrospect that can invest
the occasions with any significance. Indeed, there is nothing to indicate that those first meetings were anything but casual, and due more
to Yeats's friendship with the Anglo-Parisian symbolist-critic Arthur
Symons than to anything else. It was in fact Symons who occasioned
Yeats's first meeting with Lady Gregory, for the two men had been to
stay with Edward Martyn in the west of Ireland after visiting the
Aran Islands in search of material for Yeats's novel. With true Irish
courtesy, Martyn naturally introduced his distinguished guests to his
neighbour at Coole. Later that year Yeats and Symons were in Paris,
again on a cultural tour (they were present at the first production of
Alfred Jarry's *Ubu Roi*), admittedly not unmixed with nationalist
fervour, for among other things Yeats was in pursuit of Maud Gonne.
Informed that there was another Irish writer in residence, and piqued
because he did not know him, Yeats introduced himself to John Synge.

Time and Willie Yeats have endowed both meetings with the
mystique of revelation, Yeats the leading actor on centre stage. Cer-

tainly in less than a year he had made the first of his visits to Coole
Park where, since he already considered himself a practising dramatist, talk inevitably turned on plays. So too, in the meeting with John
Synge, the conversation was led by Yeats; his imagination still full of
the Aran Islands, and his respect for the erudition of Arthur Symons
brooking no rival, he urged Synge at a somewhat later date to give up
imitating the latter and search out the former. However, it was not
until two years later that Synge visited Aran or received his first invitation to Coole. (The Parisian aspect of Irish nationalism appears
to have affected him somewhat earlier, for preserved among his papers
at his death was a signed photograph of Maud Gonne.) This was not
a sudden mystical union of three minds, therefore, in whose blinding
flash Dublin's Temple of Art appeared behind the trembling veil. Nor,
with the exception of Lady Gregory's and Yeats's own strong bond,
was the union of hearts ever an easy one. Besides, the Abbey Theatre
stationary does not list the three directors until late in 1905. We must
look to earlier, less easy alliances, for the original ideals.

Like many another artistic and revolutionary venture, the early
impulses seem to have come, with few exceptions, from abroad; even
though, as with so many things Irish, this frequently meant a reaction
(characterised by high seriousness and supreme self-consciousness)
against those very influences. Some of this was the inevitable result of
England's smothering political and economic superiority, which forced
Irish men of letters to look across the channel not only for their audiences, but for their publishing houses. (It was not until the early years
of this century that writers of the literary movement could have their
books published in Ireland, and for some time even that possibility
was often doubtful, considering the idiosyncrasies of George Roberts
and the House of Maunsel.) But more so, it was the outcome of centuries of cosmopolitanism, which made Dublin at once a narrow pro-
vincial city and the second cultural centre of the Empire. Added to
these factors, consider the traditions of Ireland's 'Wild Geese' – who
(in this period at any rate) lived for the most part comfortably and

bilingually in Paris – and the 'Returned Yanks' – who further promoted dreams of remote and golden possibilities. The first issue of
Beltaine, published in 1899, proclaimed its manifesto in no narrow
parochial terms: 'The Irish Literary Theatre will attempt to do in
Dublin something of what has been done in London and Paris.' The
founders of this new project clearly wished to identify themselves with
international as well as national movements.

Ironically, it was not until Synge became a director that this internationalism was denounced, when the most European of them all
roundly turned upon his fellow directors for assuming that 'the con-
tinental municipal theatre' was the pattern they should aim for.[4] But
ten years earlier, with Synge safely ensconced in the Sorbonne study-
ing Breton, and James Joyce, still ignorant of Nora Barnacle, reading
his Ibsen in the National Library, to most Irishmen England was
fairyland.[5] And the members of that first dramatic triumvirate, Yeats,
Martyn, and Moore (for Lady Gregory was at first only the secretary),
had for many years lived in the centre of that kingdom. Notwithstand-
ing the steady pressures from beyond the channel, then, it is to London
that we must first turn for the earliest signs of the dramatic revival in
Ireland.

London itself was a whirlpool of new ideas and fresh evaluations of
all aspects of art, and it was these restless tributaries rather than the
general stream the young men from Ireland chose to explore. In some
cases the exploration led to extraordinary feats of adaptation.
Although William Morris, for example, would doubtless approve of
the Dun Emer and Cuala Presses – had not his daughter May taught
the Yeats sisters embroidery and French? – and excited the young
poet by his self-commending approval – 'You write my sort of poetry,"
it is doubtful whether he would have recognised John Ball's dream in
the romance of the beggarman, to say nothing of the noble. And Morris
would have been somewhat puzzled too by being yoked with Richard
Wagner as creators of the 'new romance' in Celtic literature.[7] But
although to Yeats, as to Bernard Shaw, he remained chief of men,[8]

Morris's direct influence waned in favour of younger ideas. More directly of use were the stylish tenets of Oscar Wilde who, Max Beerbohm reminds us, 'first trotted' the Ideal of Beauty round the suburbs of Chelsea.[9] And Shaw wickedly pointed out that William Butler Yeats, appearing on the London scene shortly after the success of Gilbert and Sullivan's *Patience*, proved Wilde's point that nature copies art.[10] For the aesthetic movement satirised in *Patience* assumed great importance for Yeats and his fellow Islanders. The accent on sensation and emotion expressed in a personal language is reflected both in the symbolism of Yeats's early poetry and, in the life of George Moore, the desire to 'épater le bourgeois.' Yeats was not altogether averse to this second quality himself, for he writes to John O'Leary of his theatrical enterprise with Florence Farr, 'She is desirous of doing my next play as it is a wild mystical thing carefully arranged to be an insult to the regular theatregoer who is hated by both of us.'[11] The importance of ritual and form encouraged Yeats's already avid interest in mysticism as much as it satisfied Edward Martyn's Oxford Catholicism. And the constant search for earlier models and fresh material encouraged a 'Celtic revival' by no means limited to Ireland. The peculiar combination of mysticism and celticism in Yeats during those years prompted one Dublin critic to comment accurately if maliciously that Yeats's 'occult mission, it seemed, was to celebrate the wedding of Madame Blavatsky and Finn MacCumhail.'[12] Furthermore, although the aesthetes' concern for style did much to heighten the subjective Yeats's awareness of his need for a pose – no matter how genuine – and a mission – no matter how difficult – the intensity and self-absorption of the artists of the nineties encouraged his determination to fight for his own dream, however unpopular. Later he was to defend this intellectual arrogance in a quarrel with AE over theatre affairs : 'I desire the love of a very few people, my equals or my superiors. The love of the rest would be a bond and an intrusion. These others will in time come to know that I am a fairly strong and capable man and that I have gathered the strong and capable about me, and all who love work better than idle talk will support me. It is a long fight but that is the sport of it.'[13]

But when Yeats wrote this letter to AE in 1906, he was firmly established in his own organisation, housed in a building provided for his use and the propagation of his ideals, encouraged by an Irish aristocrat and financed by an English heiress. He could in all confidence continue his letter, 'I know quite well ... I will never have the support of the clubs. ... The only question with me (and it is one I have argued with Synge and Lady Gregory) is whether I should attack the clubs openly.' But in London in 1891 (the year Conor Cruise O'Brien has called the beginning of 'an interval between a verdict and a sentence'[14]) the younger, less-confident poet was anxiously seeking, even originating, societies in which he could feel that support. That year he joined at least two clubs. One was the Rhymers' Club, founded under his auspices with the help of two other anglicised Celts, Ernest Rhys and T. W. Rolleston, where in their search for 'the Mystical in Art'[15] the young poets of the Cheshire Cheese could raise poetry to the tradition of a religion and life itself to the eminence of ritual. The second, again with Rolleston, was the London Irish Literary Society. Yeats had already been for some time a member of the Order of the Golden Dawn and a few years later was to join Maud Gonne in the Irish Republican Brotherhood. After first founding the London branch of the Irish Literary Society, he tackled Dublin, offering as bait a new Library of Ireland with books and lectures which would 'endeavour to make the patriotism of the people who read them both deeper and more enlightened, and ... set before them the national and legendary heroes as they present themselves to the minds of scholars and thinkers.'[16] By the time control of the National Literary Society and its New Irish Library had passed from his hands, he had added a third interest to 'management of men' – 'theatre business' – and planned with his fellow member of the Golden Dawn, Florence Farr, the establishment of 'a small literary theatre' in the suburbs of London. Except for Miss Farr's production of *The Land of Heart's Desire* (poster by the aesthete Beardsley, patronage by Miss Horniman of the Golden Dawn), this theatre never materialised, but by then Yeats had come to realise that only on the stage could he achieve his public role.

Plays were indeed in the air. Impressed by his visits to Antoine's Theatre in Paris, George Moore had enthusiastically recommended to the English public the foundation of its own Théâtre Libre and – again in 1891 – participated in the founding of the Independent Theatre Society. The impact on the English public of their first productions, Ibsen's *Ghosts* and Zola's *Thérèse Raquin,* has been adequately described by Bernard Shaw, a new playwright 'discovered' by the Independent Theatre the following year; but the memory of those riotous performances lingered long not only in Shaw's and Moore's memories but also in Yeats's. Later he was to look with satisfaction upon Synge as 'his' Ibsen. Other theatrical experiments followed, and the possibility of a national theatre in England was voiced. All were concerned, like their French prototypes (Antoine's Théâtre Libre, Lugné-Poë's Théâtre d'Art), with the encouragement of playwrights and enriched possibilities for the actor. All looked upon the general public as a thing to be tolerated and educated, or, if proved uneducable and financially unnecessary, ignored. As the result of a wager, Moore himself presented a problem play, which he hopefully considered to be in the manner of Ibsen, and *The Strike at Arlingford* appeared the same year as Yeats's first play. Moore's cousin Martyn followed suit, but, alas for Edward, no English company would accept either the Ibsenite *Heather Field* or the Celtic *Maeve.* (Surprisingly, AE possessed a copy of *A Doll's House* as early as 1891.)

Ibsen was not wholeheartedly accepted by all the young men of the nineties, for he had a strong rival in the current vogue for Wagnerism, and few could rationalise the two loves as cleverly as Bernard Shaw. Arthur Symons preferred Wagner's method of expressing 'the subconscious life' with heroic characters and 'continuous unresolved melody' to the 'too probable people' of Ibsen's plays, who, he complained, 'speak a language exactly on the level of their desks and their shop-counters' (a criticism Yeats and Lady Gregory were to raise of the Cork realists of their own movement some fifteen years later). Yeats charitably admitted the similarity of aim in attempting to achieve a new theatre of beauty based on contemporary actuality (or as Lady Gregory was to say in deprecating her own contributions, 'a theatre with a base of realism, an apex of beauty'), but could not feel that Ibsen's means justified Yeats's ends. He could never forgive the 'stale odour of spilt poetry' in William Archer's 'hygienic' translations.[17] To the Celt who had the glories of ancient heroes as models, Ibsen's characters were imprisoned in their commonplace circumstances and everyday language. Synge, reading Ibsen in an even stodgier German translation, complained on much the same grounds, disowning the 'joyless and pallid words' of Ibsen and Zola, although a later unpublished farce acknowledges that he and Ibsen were fighting for the same liberties. And the influence of Ibsen clung to every theatre movement that followed, contributing, as we shall see, to the collapse of the first Irish triumvirate while strengthening the resolve of the second.

While Florence Farr was producing *The Land of Heart's Desire* at the Avenue Theatre, yet one further organisation was making its impact on the poet-playwrights of London. For in that year William Poel founded the Elizabethan Stage Society in an attempt to bring back to the stage a more sincere, hence less ostentatious, reproduction of the dramatist's intentions. For Poel, everything in the theatre was subordinate to the spoken word : all voices must be orchestrated (a principle Shaw followed throughout his theatrical career) and all art founded on repose (perhaps his greatest single influence on the Fay brothers). Shakespeare's language required, Poel felt, 'tuned tones' and 'an exaggerated naturalness,' by which he meant an inflected speech which, rather than distorting the language, simply exaggerated the elements already there. The staging must remain as unobtrusive as possible.

Yeats was also impressed by John Todhunter's similar experiments with poetic drama in a small clubhouse in Bedford Park. He reviewed them for *The Boston Pilot* during his brief journalist career in the 1890s, commenting on the 'semi-religious effect new to the modern stage' achieved by Todhunter's 'sonorous verse, united to the rhythmical motions of the white-robed chorus, and the solemnity of burning incense.' No wonder he was to write to AE a few years later, 'the magical word is the chanted word.' Furthermore, Todhunter's play appealed, he proclaimed to his American audience, to 'that circle of cultivated people who remain faithful to the rightful Muses, and have not bowed the knee to those two slatterns, farce and melodrama.'[18] Seventeen years later, although having flirted perilously with both these slatterns in his own theatre, he was to use the same arrogant phrasing and pretentious tone in his defence of the artist against the public. As early as 1891, with Todhunter and William Poel as examples before him, he had already decided that 'People needed, coming fresh from the trivialities of the world of shops and tea tables, the "once upon a time" that begins the make-believe of fairy tales. ... Once get your audience in that mood, and you can do anything with it.'[19] One is reminded of the principle to be practised by the Irish Theatre: in Lady Gregory's words, 'We went on giving what we thought good until it became popular.'[20] (It is interesting to note the similarity in aim between Yeats and that other didactic, magical playwright, Bernard Shaw, who aimed for 'the melting mood' although by a different route.)

This new approach to the drama in England demanded, then, first a new method of speaking verse, and secondly, a different attitude towards stage decoration. Yeats became directly involved in experiments in both. Prominent among the speech reformers was Florence Farr, who had acted in Todhunter's pastoral drama, *A Sicilian Idyll*, written on a subject suggested by Yeats, and had collaborated with Poel in the Elizabethan Stage Society; she was to produce plays by both Shaw and Yeats, and as gossip would have it she had already initiated both dramatists into more of life's mysteries than the Golden

Dawn. Yeats was impressed by her verse-speaking, which, he felt, gave the poetry 'a nobility, a passionate austerity that made it akin for certain moments to the great poetry of the world.' 'I had discovered for the first time,' he was to write in his *Autobiographies*, 'that in the performance of all drama that depends for its effect upon beauty of language, poetical culture may be more important than professional experience.'[21] On this principle he was later to welcome the young Dublin players trained by Frank Fay, and win the approval of the London critics when the Irish company visited England for the first time. Although other interests led Yeats and Miss Farr further apart, their partnership in searching for a universal method of declaiming and musically annotating verse continued for some twenty years; in 1909 Yeats was still sufficiently involved in the experiments to write to her of 'our method,' and frequently throughout the early years of the Abbey Theatre Florence Farr was asked to cross to Dublin for a training session with the players. When, in January 1899, the Irish Literary Theatre was founded under the auspices of the National Literary Society, Florence Farr was elected general manager; four months later she created the part of the poet Aleel in the Literary Theatre's first production, *The Countess Cathleen*. Meanwhile in Dublin Frank Fay was becoming more and more fanatic in his pronouncements, both in his newspaper articles and to his young pupils, on verse-speaking in the William Poel manner. When the Fays finally left the Abbey Theatre in 1908, it was William Poel the directors first turned for advice in training the actors, and, in turn, Poel was happy to make use of the golden voice of Sara Allgood, trained by Frank Fay.

To these examples we could add the important but generally under-rated influence of Gordon Craig and Charles Ricketts on Yeats's concept of staging and design.[22] Himself a painter, Yeats became increasingly conscious of the need for simplification of staging, so deliberately at variance with the productions in the commercial London theatres. The experiments of Gordon Craig under his mother

Ellen Terry's benevolent management in London excited not only Yeats but Willie Fay, who was so impressed by Craig's lecture on 'The Reform of the Theatre'[23] that he ordered a model theatre for himself. Later, Craig designed several Abbey Theatre productions and gave the company first opportunity to use his screens and masks. Charles Ricketts, although he never visited Dublin, willingly contributed suggestions, working methods, and costume and scenic designs whenever necessary.

But such examples of international cross-fertilisation could be continued indefinitely, and so let us turn once again to Dublin, with the further reminder that Moore, like Synge, studied first in Paris, that Martyn, like Shaw, was an avid Wagnerian, that Lady Gregory was a constant visitor to Italy (one of her first articles on the theatre described the acting of Eleanora Duse), and that Florence Farr eventually became so involved with Eastern philosophy that she left England to teach in a Buddhist school in Ceylon.

'The modern Irish theatre began,' asserts Bernard Shaw in 'A Note on Aggressive Nationalism,' 'with the *Cathleen ni Houlihan* of Mr Yeats and Lady Gregory's *Rising of the Moon*, in which the old patriotism stirred and wrung its victims; but when the theatre thus established called on Young Ireland to write Irish plays and found a national school of drama, the immediate result was a string of plays of Irish life – and very true to life they were – in which the heroines proclaimed that they were sick of Ireland and rated their Nationalist husbands for sacrificing all the realities of life to senseless Fenian maunderings, and the heroes damned Ireland up hill and down dale in the only moments of enthusiasm their grey lives left possible.'[24]

Certainly the new dramatic movement in Ireland during the 1890s could not have arrived at a more opportune moment. Political nationalism of the Thomas Davis kind was passing, leaving in its place a temporary patriotism roused from apathy by a spirit more of reaction and criticism than of construction and creation. A revival of Irish scholarship did much to fill this vacuum, and the lofty ideals of the old Fenian John O'Leary inspired the young people around him to a new enthusiasm, that of Irish folklore and history. 'There are things a man must not do to save a nation,' O'Leary had warned, and gradually though perhaps only faintly alongside the militant Fenianism of a few diehard newspapers, there came a plea for dignity, for intellectual freedom, for allegiance to the few who might share a common artistic aim. It was perhaps of this spirit that Yeats was thinking when he wrote of his audience in *Discoveries* in 1906, 'I had not wanted to "elevate them" or "educate them," as these words are understood, but to make them understand my vision, and I had not wanted a large audience, certainly not what is called a national audience, but enough people for what is incidental and temporary to lose itself in the lump.' Lady Gregory, somewhat more graciously, referred to the task of restoring to Ireland 'its ancient dignity.' There were already moves in this direction, for in 1892, before the newly formed Irish National Literary Society of Dublin, Douglas Hyde delivered a lecture on 'the necessity for de-Anglicising Ireland.' The following year he founded the Gaelic League, whose aim was not so much 'getting rid of English but at "keeping Irish spoken where it is spoken still." ' (Shaw claimed that even the Gaelic League began 'in Bedford Park, London, W., after a prolonged incubation in Somerset House.'[25] (The new interest in the Irish Celt was infectious. At the height of his Irish enthusiasm George Moore threatened to disown his brother's children (having none to acknowledge himself) if they did not immediately learn to speak Irish, and Edward Martyn was for many years a member of the governing body of the Gaelic League. Lady Gregory and her son Robert became interested in the language under the influence of Hyde and the encouragement of Martyn, and even Synge won the Irish medal at Trinity College. (However, Synge's early training in that language seems to have been mainly the result of proselytising church groups who donated the Irish bibles used as texts in TCD, and although he was proud of his own Gaelic heritage, he dismissed the Irish of the Gaelic League as 'incoherent twaddle.') Whatever the varying reactions to the Gaelic League, it did much to stimulate interest in Irish mythology and literature, and on a much more practical scale for our purposes, acted as the catalyst which provided the first triumvirate with native actors.

We are all familiar with the various metamorphoses through which the Irish Literary Theatre passed before it became the Company of Irish Players at the Abbey Theatre, Dublin, some ten years later. Early in 1897 Yeats had written to Fiona Macleod from Paris, where he was once again trying to start a branch of the Young Ireland Society: 'Our Irish Literary and Political literary organisations are pretty complete. ... and I think it would be very possible to get up Celtic plays through these Societies. They would be far more effective than lectures and might do more than anything else we can do to make the Irish, Scotch and other Celts recognise their solidarity. ... If we have one or two short direct prose plays of (say) a mythological and folklore kind ... I feel sure we could get the Irish Literary Society to make a start.'[26] Fortunately Lady Gregory persuaded Yeats to change his original suggested title from 'Sharp-ridden Celtic' to the Irish Literary Theatre, and it was under that banner that the first manifesto, an appeal to guarantors (culled mainly from Lady Gregory's Protestant Ascendancy friends who were accustomed to humouring her enthusiasms), was published later that year. Some eighteen months later still, sufficient funds had been raised (generously guaranteed by Edward Martyn) and a company formed (vigorously collected in London by George Moore) to produce Yeats's *Countess Cathleen* and Martyn's *Heather Field*, under the benevolent if patronising eye of Dublin's National Literary Society. A small organised claque of 'Davis nationalists' attempted to interrupt the performance of Yeats's play, but Joseph Holloway records with satisfaction their complete frustration by the enthusiastic applause 'which drowned their empty-headed expressions of dissension.'[27] Indeed, whatever slight disturbance occurred on opening night was nothing to the tempest created by the nationalist press, which quoted from a pamphlet *Souls for Gold* which in turn quoted from an earlier published version of the play, and by Yeats's fellow director Martyn, whose Catholic conscience required two outside readers and a promise of absolution to console him.

The experiment of the Irish Literary Theatre continued for three years, adding George Moore and further dissent, this time concentrated between directors, when Moore was called in to rewrite poor Edward's second Ibsenite drama. A definite Celtic emphasis was added by Martyn's dream play *Maeve* (which was not a success) and Alice Milligan's Ossianic tableau, *The Last Feast of the Fianna* ('picturesque,' grunted Holloway, but 'the actors weren't as good as the ladies'). During the third year, the Gaelic League took over not only in spirit but in performance. Frank Benson's English company, suffering from the natural distortion of unfamiliar Irish names, stumbled through Moore and Yeats's ill-fated *Diarmuid and Grania*, while a company of Dublin amateurs, the author in the leading role, romped successfully in Douglas Hyde's little Irish play *The Twisting of the Rope*. In contrast to the 'English' funeral music composed by Edward Elgar for the first play, the audience sang old Irish airs during the interval; later for a French magazine Synge recalled his own emotion on hearing the old songs of Ireland sung spontaneously, perhaps for the first time, in the Irish language by such a large public gathering. 'On venait de sentir flotter un instant dans la salle l'âme d'un peuple.'[28] The founders of the Irish Literary Theatre could indeed look with satisfaction upon the success of their three-year experiment, but meanwhile Edward Martyn and George Moore had served their turn. Martyn was dissatisfied with the 'narrow aims' of the movement; drama for him meant international plays established on Ibsenite principles. Moore, a man of many enthusiasms (but only one at a time, as Beerbohm reminds us), had become slightly tired of the theatre and, bored by Yeats and the Irish movement, transformed his idolatry to an embarrassed AE.

Neither Yeats nor Lady Gregory was disturbed by the withdrawal of their partners; if anything, they were relieved. They had begun to realise that help must come from within, and the small company of amateurs who had performed with the author in the little Gaelic play were themselves looking for support. Yeats wrote to Lady Gregory early in March of a request from a priest – a friend of AE's – for an Irish passion play; that summer the small company, under the direction of W. G. Fay, a professional actor who had been performing for some time in music hall farces round Ireland, produced another play in Irish (incidentally by another priest). The actors, stage-managed by Willie, trained in voice and gesture by his brother Frank, were nationalist members of Willie Fay's 'Comedy Combination' and later 'Ormonde Dramatic Society,' and artistically inclined members of Inghinidhe na hEireann (The Daughters of Erin), a nationalist organisation actively sponsored by Maud Gonne. Doubtless urged on by Miss Gonne, Yeats had already formed a liaison with members of the company, inviting them to join a committee to publicise the third and final season of the Literary Theatre and to work towards an Irish National Theatre.[29] James Cousins, one of the committee members, discovered one act of AE's *Deirdre* and persuaded the Angelic Anarchist to complete the play. AE in turn suggested to Lady Gregory that Yeats contribute *Cathleen ni Houlihan*; he was abetted by Maud Gonne, who agreed to play the title role. The company became W. G. Fay's Irish National Dramatic Society when both plays were produced in the spring of 1902.

We need not follow in such detail the next phases of this movement towards an Irish theatre, except to admire the delicacy with which the struggles for power resulted in victory for Yeats and his colleagues. There appears to have been little or no formal organisation of Fay's Society. Willie and Frank Fay sought out the plays, which on the whole were provided by enthusiastic actors already in the company. Funds for the rehearsal hall and costumes were donated by interested members who also cheerfully built the sets; talk turned on 'the movement' although no particular direction seemed to be headed for; and

Frank Fay scolded all within hearing on proper speech and gesture. Meanwhile Yeats and Lady Gregory contemplated a further issue of *Beltaine* (retitled *Samhain*), kept in touch with Synge, collaborated on *A Pot of Broth*, and watched the small group's preparations with interest. Lady Gregory wrote to Yeats, 'If you want any movement to succeed, you must use all sorts,' but left for Italy before the first performance of their *Cathleen ni Houlihan*. The players felt vaguely uneasy when Yeats congratulated them with the words, 'Splendid. Beautiful verse beautifully spoken by native actors. Just what we wanted.'[30] By August of 1902 Yeats and AE had persuaded them that a definite organisation was necessary. The Irish National Theatre Society was formed, with Yeats as president, Maud Gonne, Douglas Hyde, and AE as vice-presidents, W. G. Fay as stage manager, and Fred Ryan, one of the actor-authors, as secretary. Everyone had equal vote, and everyone decided on choice of plays. Within a year Yeats provided two more plays, Lady Gregory wrote her first, and John Synge had joined the movement. Again dissension arose, as patriotism vied with artistic considerations in the choice of plays. Maud Gonne and two of the principal players staged a public walk-out when *The Shadow of the Glen* was performed; Yeats battled noisily, furiously, and successfully to reject a bad play by James Cousins. Meanwhile the Society became even more self-conscious and serious, when in May 1903 they visited London under the auspices of the Irish Literary Society. Frank Fay became even more concerned about the company's acting, Yeats more alarmed by the possibilities of losing artistic control. He contributed another play, as did Synge and Lady Gregory. Still he and the Fays, who agreed with him, could be outvoted. Finally, after a second visit to London, Yeats played his trump card – he produced Miss Horniman. By the end of 1904 the company was in the Abbey Theatre; but the letter from Miss Horniman offering support was to Yeats, not to the company, and in support of artistic and dramatic aims 'as publicly explained by you on various occasions.' By September of the following year the National Theatre Society had become a limited company, with three directors, Yeats, Lady Gregory, and Synge, Willie Fay as stage manager, and Frank Fay as secretary. More actors left, as did some of the playwrights. Encouraged by AE and Padraic Colum, the separatists formed a rival company, The Theatre of Ireland; but patriotism was no satisfactory exchange for literary aims, and it was many years before the Abbey Theatre had a successful rival.

The pattern of these early struggles repeated itself again and again in the history of the Abbey Theatre, each time the Reproof Valiant giving way rapidly to the Countercheck Quarrelsome. With each battle we can see the early ideals attempting, not always successfully, to cope with the rising tide of indignant patriotism on the one hand, personal ambition on the other. Frequently one characteristic carried with it the destruction of another. The struggle for control between the officers of the company and the earlier patriotic groups of actors led in turn to a struggle for power between Willie Fay and the actors; the Fays left. Many years later Yeats was to admit, 'I am no Nationalist, except in Ireland for passing reasons,'[31] but that nationalism in Ireland, necessary to the foundation of a theatre established on Irish principles, led in turn to a split with Miss Horniman and the loss of her subsidy. The need to keep the theatre open on a commercial basis frequently meant the acceptance of substandard Irish plays which the company could easily perform and produce, so that there would be trained actors when more artistically ambitious plays appeared. More and more often Yeats had to look elsewhere for actresses and producers who could do justice to his own verse plays. Before his death Synge himself, perhaps the most fortunate in matching players to play, had become disenchanted with the company. Frequently Lady Gregory would become disheartened, fearing they were 'humouring' their audience instead of 'educating' it to 'Art and a thinking Democracy.' The greater their need for fresh playwrights, the less able they were to cater to the strong plays they were offered: Shaw wrote *John Bull's Other Island* for them, but the play was rejected; George Fitzmaurice contributed his wild fantasies, but they were misunderstood by players and audience alike; James Joyce offered them *Exiles,* but the company was out in the music halls; later, the directors balked at O'Casey's challenge. Occasionally the directors themselves disagreed past the Retort Courteous: Yeats had angrily to remind Synge of his duties to the theatre his plays were in danger of wrecking; on various occasions Lady Gregory felt compelled to recall her colleagues to those *Samhain* principles of 'good playwriting, good speaking, good acting and the scenic art.' In 1919 Yeats, realising that it had become a 'People's Theatre,' publicly admitted that the Abbey Theatre experiment was a failure in his terms while a success in national terms. But miraculously, the movement survived the ravages of audience, company, directors. When in 1924 Yeats received the Nobel Prize, he chose to accept it in the name of his fellow directors and his theatre. When old age and rheumatism prevented Lady Gregory from regular attendance, she could note with satisfaction in her diary a 'splendid' performance of 'a fine play,' in 'a Theatre of our own.'

Holloway's diary for 1905 records Yeats's remark about *On Baile's Strand* in terms of the story of Parnell: 'People who do aught for Ireland ever and always have to fight with the waves in the end.'[32] It might not be too fanciful to read into the directors' own choice of themes an accurate reflection of the unending struggles of the Irish dramatic movement: the poet Seanchan fights for his rights with the King, the Playboy battles constantly with his Da, Hyacinth Halvey is forever lumbered by the reputation he so painstakingly created.

'Intellectual hatred' and 'intellectual nationalism': the paradox of passionate politics

GEORGE MILLS HARPER

Although Yeats apparently decided early in his career that 'there is no fine literature without nationality,'[1] he was not always certain what nationality meant or what methods patriotic Irishmen should employ to achieve national freedom. He was, of course, consistently concerned with the mythopoeic function of nationality in literature rather than the usefulness of literature as propaganda for nationalistic doctrines. It was that issue which led to his controversy with the Dublin press in the early days of the Irish National Theatre. Arthur Griffith, in *The United Irishman*, was the most vociferous spokesman for the popular patriotic stance: 'Did I tell you,' Yeats wrote to Lady Gregory, 'my idea of challenging Griffith to debate with me in public our two policies – his that literature should be subordinate to nationalism, and mine that it must have its own ideal? I think that a challenge to him would be quite amusing, for his own party sent out so many that he would be a little embarrassed to refuse. I would offer to debate it with him or any other person appointed by his societies.'[2] It is not my purpose here to consider the issue of this proposed debate, but rather to point out the gradual emergence of two opposed nationalistic viewpoints and to suggest that Yeats's choice of one over the other was, as Blake would have said, 'uneasy' because he had inclinations towards both. I will suggest also that the great art which developed from his intellectual nationalism would not have been possible without the abrasive stimulant of its opposite, the intellectual hatred of the revolutionaries and the secret societies. Yeats himself vacillated, especially during the nineties. He joined the IRB, and 'went hither and thither speaking at meetings in England and Scotland and occasionally at tumultuous Dublin conventions, and endured some of the worst months of my life.'³ But he came to fear the 'movement of abstraction and hatred' (A360) which possessed the other party. 'I dreaded some wild Fenian movement,' he recalled, 'and with litera-ture perhaps more in my mind than politics, dreamed of that Unity of Culture which might begin with some few men controlling some form of administration' (A362).

We ought to be grateful, I suppose, that Yeats was a divided man – most great artists are. He was a man of paradoxes and tensions and uncertainties, not the least of which is the ambivalent stance he took on Irish politics. He had learned from William Blake, if he needed a teacher, that 'Without Contraries is no progression.'

Although Yeats insisted throughout much of his life that he was an intellectual nationalist with little interest in practical politics, he was in fact obsessed with the subject and sought to create art out of the paradox suggested in these polar opposites, both of which appealed to him. To the public, however, he consistently projected himself as the representative of one pole in diametric opposition to an important but misguided segment of Irish writers and politicians, and the two groups were finally engaged in an increasingly great struggle for the minds and loyalties of the unthinking body politic. In a very real sense almost all his work after the death of Parnell is an attempt to mould the seemingly intractable material of propaganda into living form.

But it might never have become art if the opposition had not been epitomised in Maud Gonne. She was most likely right in her shrewd judgment that Yeats would have been a lesser poet without her opposi-tion, without which, by his own testament, 'I might have thrown poor words away/And been content to live.'[4] As poet and artist he preferred contemplation; as ardent suitor and student of politics he yearned for action.

To students of literature, it is exciting to imagine what Yeats might have become if Maud had yielded to his entreaties. Would 'my movement,' as he called his quest for 'Unity of Culture,' have failed utterly without the leadership he provided? Or was it inevitable that the public stance he assumed should find a champion? Or would he have become an even greater artist through union with his ideological opposite? Such speculations are obviously futile, if not utterly fruitless; and I have no intention of trying to imagine the prayer he might have made for his daughter if Maud had become the mother instead of 'an old bellows full of angry wind.' Rather, I propose to trace Yeats's own ambivalence towards Maud and Irish nationalism, and to chart briefly his vacillating course in what he was to call the 'labour of politics.' I want to suggest also the point of view and perhaps counter-ambivalence of Maud, who stood at times for 'intellectual hatred' at its worse, but who was not the only one around with an 'opinionated mind.' Although most students and critics are readily convinced that Yeats overcame accursed opinions, we must remember that he was constantly besieged by them and would not in all likelihood have been the great poet he became if he had not been forced to struggle. At any rate, it is revealing to watch the battle as he recorded it in action and words.

We may begin with Yeats's vacillation and uncertainty about the Young Irelanders. He was, as he tells us, led to read them through John O'Leary, whose favourite apparently was the national favourite, Thomas Davis; and the source of Yeats's factual information was Gavan Duffy's *Young Ireland* (1880). Duffy was biased, having quarrelled with John Mitchel, the finest writer and most impassioned of the leaders. Whether or not Yeats would have chosen Davis over Mitchel if he had not learned through Duffy, the fact is that Yeats's choice was deliberate. Speaking in 1914 at the Davis centenary meeting in Dublin, Yeats concluded that 'the political influence of Mitchel ... has been almost wholly mischievous,' and Yeats's reason is important : 'Mitchel played upon international suspicion and exalted the hate of England above the love of Ireland that Davis would have taught us, and his gaping harpies are on our roof-tree now.'[5] In his bitter moments, Yeats must have listed Maud among the harpies and traced her intellectual hatred to the school of Mitchel.

Although the Young Irelanders as a group found a *raison d'être* in their opposition to O'Connell's policies, including his insistence on non-violence, Davis belonged to the coterie of Gavan Duffy, who ultimately split with John Mitchel over the issue of armed revolt. In the words of Duffy, Davis had 'no faith in the Gallic bravado ... of baptising the cause in blood.' Like Yeats, he feared mob violence and murder : 'The people of Munster are starving,' he wrote; 'Will murder feed them?' And like Yeats also, he had faith in the 'Aristocracy of Ireland.'[6] To Padraic Pearse, the intellectual nationalist of the Easter Revolution, Davis was 'the first of modern Irishmen to make explicit the truth that nationality is a spirituality.'[7] As a proponent of cultural unity, Davis wanted 'not a Nationality which would prelude civil war, but which would establish internal independence – a Nationality which would be recognised by the world and sanctioned by wisdom, virtue and prudence.'[8] Even Arthur Griffith, who sided with Maud and opposed Yeats, praised this strain in Davis : 'When the Irish read and reflect with Davis,' he wrote, 'their day of redemption will be at hand.'[9]

Of course, such remarks reflect the generalities and abstractions which irritated Yeats and his followers. But there was a side to Davis which clearly set him off from most of the Young Irelanders and suggested him as the model for O'Leary first, then Yeats and his circle; more than any of the others Davis hoped for Ireland's salvation through unity of culture. When Douglas Hyde and Father Michael O'Hickey organised the Gaelic League, they found the perfect expression of their plan 'to cultivate everything that is most racial, most

Gaelic, most Irish' in words of Thomas Davis: 'Nationality ... is the summary name for many things. It seeks a literature made by Irishmen, and coloured by our scenery, manners and character. It desires to see art applied to express Irish thoughts and belief. It would make our music sound in every parish at twilight, our pictures sprinkle the walls of every house, and and our poetry and history sit at every hearth. It would thus create a race of men full of more intensely Irish character and knowledge, and to that race it would give Ireland.'[10] Even more like Yeats's thought was the toast Davis proposed at the first banquet of the '82 Club for 'The Advancement of the Fine Arts in Ireland.' 'There is a close connection between National Art and National Independence. Art is the born foe of slavery and of the friends of slavery – of ignorance, of sensuality and of cowardice. ... How can he who never heard the shout of freeman ... reach the form of a great artist?'[11] Although Yeats was an artist first and a nationalist second, whereas Davis was a nationalist who cultivated the arts for his purpose, it is clear that Yeats learned much from Davis.

But he was torn between Davis's intellectual nationalism and John Mitchel's 'pure hatred to England,' which, as Mitchel suggested to himself in a wellknown passage in the *Jail Journal*, was 'a diseased longing for blood and carnage.' 'And for the *chance* of getting Ireland severed from England in the dreadful *mêlée*,' his Doppelganger asks, 'do you desire to see all Europe and America plunged in desperate war?'[12] Almost any student of Yeats will respond to that question with his famous line from Mitchel's prayer: 'Send war in our time, O Lord!' (v638). At times, certainly, perhaps all his life, Yeats was quite sympathetic to Mitchel's strain of nationalistic fervour, the slogan for which, according to a British historian, 'was "barricades and incendiarism," a tradition of street warfare which found belated expression in the Irish Rebellion of 1916.'[13]

Although many of the Young Irelanders ultimately sided with Mitchel, he was the leader in the break with Duffy, and in the beginning he stood almost alone. When he stopped writing for *The Nation* in late 1847, Mitchel informed Duffy that 'the present policy of *The Nation* does not suit me.' A few months later he was making it absolutely clear that he would 'belong to no society where I cannot express sentiments in favour of absolute tenant-right, and where I cannot recommend the only known method of establishing that right, namely *armed opinion*.'[14] In a 'Letter to Farmers,' written from Newgate Prison, Mitchel declared that 'Moral Force and "Patience and Perseverance" are scattered to the wild winds of Heaven. The music my countrymen now love best to hear is the rattle of arms and the ring of the rifle,' and he looked forward to 'the crash of the downfall of the thrice-accursed British Empire.'[15] In the words of Countess Markievicz, Mitchel was a 'queer mixture': 'The oddest thing about him was that he was against the freeing of the black slaves in America. Of course his reason was that the English were on the other side.' But she liked 'his ideas for Ireland' and called him 'one of the Divine Ancestors of Easter Week.'[16] To Padraic Pearse, likewise, 'Mitchel was of the stuff of which the great prophets and ecstatics have been made. He did really hold converse with God; he did really deliver God's word to man, delivered it fiery tongued.'[17] And Thomas Carlyle, after warning Mitchel that 'he would most likely be hanged,' comforted him with the assurance that 'they could not hang the immortal part of him.'[18] Like James Fintan Lalor, Mitchel was 'a passionate hater of tyranny under any form or sky.'[19] He was unalterably opposed to any compromise with England, declaring early in his career 'that Irish representation in a London Parliament is worse than useless, and that that Parliament is absolutely *nothing* to Ireland save "an engine of corruption, a workshop of coercion, and a storehouse of starvation."'[20] Of course, fiery speeches for separation were common in 1848. At one stage Mitchel and his associates became so incensed that they 'signed a pledge to refrain from the use of intoxicating drinks until the legislative independence of Ireland had been established.'[21]

The story of Mitchel's trial, conviction, and deportation is well known. It is enough, for my purpose, to point out that he became a martyr and a model, his *Jail Journal* the gospel of Irish revolution which the young Yeats, in London, read aloud for many days to his father.[22] Both the man and the book were no doubt exciting, but Yeats had discovered an even stronger attraction in John O'Leary, who had been taught by Davis rather than Mitchel: 'For all that is Irish in me,' O'Leary recalled, 'and above all, for the inspiration that made me Irish, the fountain and the origin must always be found in Davis.'[23] Years later Yeats was to pay a very similar tribute to O'Leary.

By the time Yeats met Maud Gonne, he had been exposed to both viewpoints, and had made a choice of the road to travel in carrying out 'my mission in Ireland,' but the choice had not been easy, and he was never quite sure that he had made the right choice, though he would not have been so uncertain if Maud's road had not crossed his. The stage was set for the ideological struggle at their first meeting. When she called upon Yeats at Bedford Park in London, she brought an introduction from O'Leary, under whose banner she too had enlisted, but without his cultural convictions. Maud was, in her own words, a 'one-idea'd' woman, and she constantly reminded all who cared to listen that 'there is a perpetual state of war between Ireland and England.'[24] At this meeting, Yeats recalled years later, 'She vexed my father by praise of war, war for its own sake, not as the creator of certain virtues but as if there were some virtue in excitement itself.' The love-struck Yeats supported Maud, excusing himself, in retrospect, with the observation that 'a man young as I could not have differed from a woman so beautiful and so young' (A123). Since he was temperamentally opposed to Maud's brand of politics, she brought to his life an ideological and personal tension never wholly resolved in his mind. Although Yeats also must have appeared 'one-idea'd' to the political world of Dublin, he acknowledged to himself the abiding paradox of passionate politics which he debated and projected in letters and art.

For several years after that momentous first meeting he sought to enlist Maud in the service of cultural nationalism. Feeling that 'I needed a hostess more than a society,' he wrote, 'I tried to persuade Maud Gonne to be that hostess'; but he found, alas, that 'she had already formed a new ambition, the turning of French public opinion against England' (A230). He recorded his disappointment in a harsh condemnation: 'Without intellectual freedom there can be no agreement, and in Nationalist Dublin there was not – indeed there still is not – any society where a man is heard by the right ears ... in its stead opinion crushes and rends, and all is hatred and bitterness: wheel biting upon wheel, a roar of steel or iron tackle, a mill of argument grinding all things down to mediocrity' (A230–1). Though he referred to Maud in those lines, Yeats managed as usual to include all those who disagreed with his form of nationalism. Another passage in 'Ireland after Parnell' illustrates the process of depersonalisation even better: 'When we loathe ourselves or our world, if that loathing but turn to intellect, we see self or world and its anti-self as in one vision; when loathing remains but loathing, world or self consumes itself away, and we turn to its mechanical opposite' (A234). Standing alone, of course, such oracular pronouncements seem to have little or only slight relevance to particular people, but the lines following make clear that Yeats not only is thinking of Maud as the mechanical opposite but also is suggesting that the struggle of loathing or hatred versus intellect goes on in his own mind. 'The Nationalist abstractions,' he continued, 'were like the fixed ideas of some hysterical woman, a part of the mind turned into stone, the rest a seething and burning; and Unionist Ireland had reacted from that seething and burning to a cynical indifference, and from those fixed ideas to whatever might bring the most easy and obvious success' (A234).

Yeats is, of course, recollecting events, and may be forgiven if he has over-refined the emotion rationalised in some if never complete tranquillity. But if he had written this section of his autobiography during the nineties, the tone if not the story would have been different, for he made every effort to convert Maud. He induced her to join the Theosophical Society and took her to visit Madame Blavatsky, he urged her to help him create his pseudo-political Castle of Heroes, and he sought her help in organising branches of the Young Ireland Society. But he fought a losing battle: intellectual nationalism lacked excitement for Maud, who thought the whole cultural movement somewhat ridiculous: 'Everyone must work according to his own temperament,' she recalled in after years. 'It was my philosophy of life applied to art and politics. I never willingly discouraged either a Dynamiter or a constitutionalist, a realist or a lyrical writer. My chief preoccupation was how their work could help forward the Irish Separatist movement' (178). In spite of this denial, however, she did discourage 'a lyrical writer' by her stubborn insistence that 'there must always be war till Ireland is free' (186). Maud was, in her words, 'a horse that has to wear blinkers to prevent being side-tracked – I must not look to the right or the left' (176).

She was, in fact, Yeats's opposite in many ways, and they were conscious of being antithetical complements. 'I never indulged in self-analysis,' Maud recalled, 'and often used to get impatient with Willie Yeats, who, like all writers, was terribly introspective and tried to make me so. "I have no time to think of myself," I told him which was literally true, for, unconsciously perhaps, I had redoubled work to avoid thought' (308). All the slow process of cultural change Maud was to scorn. In her opinion, the branch of the Young Ireland Society she and Yeats founded 'never did much effective work, except sending votes of congratulation (or the reverse) to political groups in Ireland' (170). Her experiment with the occult was motivated by 'the hope of gaining power to use for the great objective of my life' (256). When some of the members raised objections to her 'political activities,' she resigned. She had discovered that 'most of the members were Unionists.' They were 'strictly philosophical and non-political – which,' Maud observed, 'means non-national' in Ireland (256–7). In the meantime, 'persuaded' by Willie again, she had joined the Order of the Golden Dawn, 'where more practical magic might be learnt' (257). But the Golden Dawn was also disappointing, and when she discovered its relationship to Masonry she resigned because 'Free Masonry as we Irish know it is a British institution and has always been used politically to support the British Empire.' As a result she would 'have no connection with it.' Although 'Willie Yeats was very disappointed,' Maud was too busy for such child's play. 'They could use me,' she said; 'I could not use them. I have not time to try and learn their secrets' (259–60). It is completely appropriate that Maud should have closed the chapter about her 'Occult Experiences' with a withering observation on the Golden Dawn: 'The last authentic information I had about the Order was that they were holding ceremonies invoking peace' (260). What more was there to say!

'I have not time' is the refrain running through Maud's account of these experiences, and in fact lack of time is the chief objection to Willie's intellectual nationalism made by all who were 'Dancing to a frenzied drum' in those tempestuous and exciting years. Maud's observation about the learning of Gaelic suggests how far apart the two nationalist schools of thought were: 'Douglas Hyde ... believed in the language to free Ireland; to me the method seemed too slow; under his tuition I learned a sentence or two with which to begin my speeches, but ... I was too constantly travelling from one place to another trying to spread revolutionary thoughts and acts to sit down to the arduous task of learning a language. So Douglas Hyde never succeeded in making me an Irish speaker any more than I succeeded in making him a revolutionist' (98–9). Conscious always that the cultural nationalists 'looked down on Constance Markievicz and myself as foolish misguided women' (96), Maud would nevertheless admit that Hyde's *Literary History of Ireland* 'supplied the intellectual background of revolt' (99).

But the two groups were still searching for an ideological compromise. Maud, though 'suspect to Dublin Castle' and shadowed by two sleuths, was not yet 'on the run,' and her 'rooms over Morrow's Bookshop and Library in Nassau Street' became Dublin's intellectual pub for Yeats, Griffith, Rooney, Hyde, Connolly, McKenna, and others.

'Our talk,' Maud recalled, 'was the wine on which we used to get satisfactorily drunk. ... Many now famous poems and plays had their first reading in those rooms in Nassau Street, and many plots were hatched in them'; then she added, in a significant afterthought, 'plots for plays and plots for real life' (98). The impassioned debates about politics were clearly leading to two schools of thought with many variations. Indeed, one is tempted to conjecture that Maud's 'friends,' as she called them all, had perfect agreement on one issue alone: the necessity 'to remove from the walls various pictures of British battle-scenes' (98).

Present from the beginning, their philosophic differences led in time to an irreparable breach. Maud was on one side, Yeats on the other; and the tension must have been almost intolerable, to him at least. Maud's 'pilgrimage of passion' (84) was not to be his, but he kept hoping that they might be drawn together in the perfect cultural union: after all, he reasoned hopefully, 'A beautiful woman is always a little barbarous at heart.' When he wrote that sentence, Yeats had been talking with a French woman who was alarmed by 'the success of the anti-militarist movement.'[25] But he had as usual made the mental transfer to Maud. She was, in fact, so much on his mind that Cathleen ni Houlihan herself took on Maud's archetypal dimensions. Maud had planned to be an actress when she broke away from her family. Prevented by illness, she sought a career working for Ireland's freedom, but she never ceased acting. Although she decided that 'going on the stage is infamous' (64), she cast herself in many roles, especially Joan of Arc[26] and Cathleen ni Houlihan. As 'a servant of the Queen,' she modestly described herself as 'one of the little stones on which the feet of the Queen have rested on her way to Freedom,' but she pictured Cathleen in her own lineaments: 'Then I saw a tall, beautiful woman with dark hair blown on the wind and I knew it was Cathleen ni Houlihan. She was crossing the bog towards the hills, springing from stone to stone over the treacherous surface, and the little white stones shone, marking a path behind her, then faded into the darkness' (vii). She obviously enjoyed the legends which grew up about her: 'They are saying,' she records, 'you are a woman of the Sidhe who rode into Donegal on a white horse surrounded by birds to bring victory. No one can resist this woman' (134).

Since Yeats could not resist her, he tried conversion, but Maud was not vulnerable to his logic: 'Willie Yeats accused me of responsibility for encouraging much bad art,' she recalled, then added that she knew he would 'put up a gallant fight for good art,' and her only real concern was getting the message across (282). Yeats apparently thought of the theatre as a means of moving Maud to his viewpoint, and she stubbornly resisted, though she was willing to use the theatre to further the Nationalist movement. Three of Yeats's plays figure prominently in the tug-of-war thus set in motion: *The Countess Cathleen, The Shadowy Waters,* and *Cathleen ni Houlihan.* Although the story of *The Countess* has often been told, Maud's version has a special interest in this context. On one of those long evenings in her rooms over Morrow's Library, 'Willie Yeats had read his play, *The Countess Kathleen*; he wanted to have it produced in Dublin and he wanted me to play in it. ... I was severely tempted, for the play fascinated me and I loved acting, but just because I loved the stage so much I had made the stern resolve never to act. I was afraid it would absorb me too much to the detriment of my work. I knew my own weakness, and how, when I got interested in anything, I was capable of forgetting everything else – house-building, evicted tenants, political prisoners, even the fight against the British Empire, might all disappear in the glamour of the stage; it was the only form of self-discipline I consciously practised' (176). Maud was willing to use dramatic techniques for Ireland's cause, and even conducted a dramatic class for the Daughters of Ireland, though she refused to act in 'any of the plays we used to produce' (177). But several members of her class, including Sally and Mary Algood, did act in their plays.

On that memorable evening (Maud did not record the date) Yeats must have made his greatest effort to enlist her in the cause of intellectual nationalism, but he failed to touch her 'unshakable resolve.'

'Willie Yeats was sad,' she remembered, 'and tried hard to persuade me to act the part of Countess Kathleen. "I wrote it for you and if you don't act it we shall have to get an actress from London to take the part," which eventually he did with no marked success' (177). According to Maud, both John O'Leary and John F. Taylor, who may have been present that night, approved of her refusal to act because 'they probably understood my character and my fear of an absorption which would be detrimental to my work, in which they were interested, especially in its French side, that was beginning to be of real importance to the National struggle.' When the last of her friends left as 'the dawn was approaching,' Yeats was still determined but foiled, though, in her words, 'we were all anxious to help. It was part of the movement for capturing the intellectual life of Ireland for the National cause' (177). As usual, Maud was careful to establish the order of priority. On the same grounds also she approved the 'new clothes' Willie had put on the fairies and ancient gods, though 'the materials for these rainbow garments were not entirely of Irish weave' (178). But she was less certain of 'the mists of the Celtic Twilight which shrouded with auras many weak effusions' such as 'George Russell's bad paintings' (177).

By this time, surely, Yeats must have agreed with Aleel, in the revised version of *The Countess*, that 'Cathleen has chosen other friends than us,/And they are rising through the hollow world.' But Maud did yield to temptation just once – to play the lead in *Cathleen ni Houlihan*. Although anyone who reads *A Servant of the Queen* with some attention to Maud's delight in the sensation she was creating in Ireland as well as England and France will feel that vanity had much to do with her yielding, she felt compelled to explain her weakness in other terms: 'The only exception I ever made was when I played Cathleen ni Houlihan, and I did it because it was only on that condition that Willie Yeats would give us the right of producing his play, and I felt that play would have great importance for the National movement' (177). After all, how could she resist playing the role of 'the tall, beautiful woman with dark hair blown on the wind' (vii). Obviously this description of Queen Cathleen will serve quite as well for the Servant, as she looks in the photo of the frontispiece to Maud's book, at any rate.

Although Yeats gave *Cathleen* to the Fays instead of the Daughters of Ireland, Maud did play the lead and even brought some of her gifted Daughters into the company. If they felt 'they had given themselves up to ambition and vanity,' there is no evidence that Maud had a troubled conscience. Yeats declared that 'she made Cathleen seem like a divine being fallen into our mortal infirmity,' and induced her to become a vice-president of the Irish National Theatre.[27]

But life in the theatre was too tame for Maud, and she cared very little for any of Yeats's friends who were not *actively* engaged in the revolutionary struggle. She was glad, she said, that Yeats had found a friend in Lady Gregory, but 'feared she would take him away from the fight for Irish freedom.' Thinking of herself as Queen Cathleen, Maud contrasted Lady Gregory as 'a queer little old lady, rather like Queen Victoria.' Maud records that Lady Gregory 'had asked me if I would marry Willie Yeats. It did not seem exactly her business, and I had answered rather shortly that we were neither of the marrying sort, having other things which interested us more; and I had thought she seemed rather relieved.' Maud was suspicious of Lady Gregory's interest in 'John O'Leary's literary group,' and even of her entertainment of Willie and his friends in her Galway home: 'when these writers came back from Coole,' she observed, 'they seemed to me less passionately interested in the National struggle and more worried about their own lack of money. ... Lady Gregory and I were gracious to each other but never friends and in the later struggle in the theatre group, – Art for Art's sake or Art for Propaganda, – we were on different sides.' After 'Lady Gregory carried off Willie' to Italy, 'Willie's national outlook underwent a complete change. There would be no more poems against English kings' visits.' Willie was lost to what Maud called the 'vehement expression of Irish Independence' (332–3).

By this time, apparently, they had given up trying to convert each other, but Yeats urged the cause of union in the hope that he could thereby resolve Maud's bitter battle with the world. According to her dramatic memory, he continued to plead: 'Oh Maud, why don't you marry me and give up this tragic struggle and live a peaceful life? I could make such a beautiful life for you among artists and writers who would understand you' (329). Maud knew, of course, that neither Willie nor his friends would appreciate her brand of politics. Since her book was written long after the event, Maud was probably not as perceptive as her celebrated answer proved to be:

'Willie, are you not tired of asking that question? How often have I told you to thank the gods that I will not marry you. You would not be happy with me.'

'I am not happy without you.'

'Oh yes, you are, because you make beautiful poetry out of what you call your unhappiness and you are happy in that. Marriage would be such a dull affair. Poets should never marry. The world should thank me for not marrying you.' (329–30)

And, in fact, the world does thank Maud, for it is more true than she ever imagined that a great poet was almost literally made of his frustrated desire for 'A proud woman not kindred of his soul' (v479). Failing to enlist Maud, Yeats conceived her as his symbolic opposite, and much of the poetry after his great disappointment reflects their social and political debate and projects her image – no longer as (v149–50)

a glimmering girl
With apple blossom in her hair
Who called me by my name and ran
And faded through the brightening air

but 'A Helen of social welfare dream [who] climb[ed] on a wagonette to scream' (v626) – which is reminiscent of Miss Horniman's
wry comment that 'The greatest poet is always helpless beside a
beautiful woman screaming from a cart.'[28]

Yeats could insist in later times that 'we are the true Ireland fighting the false'[29] – meaning thereby the Abbey Theatre versus Maud's
cart – but he often seems certain that his choice is the right one only
after the alternative is impossible, that is, after Maud's marriage in
1903. Although Yeats and Maud are perhaps idealised as Aengus
and Edaine in *The Shadowy Waters*, which he continued to revise,
she has a less important place in the plays beginning with *Where There
Is Nothing*. Cathleen ni Houlihan married 'a drunken vain-glorious
lout' in February 1903; the poet reasserted his aesthetic determination, but Maud's shadow was always there. His poetry betrays Yeats's
passionate ambivalence over his forced choice : (v495)

> The intellect of man is forced to choose
> Perfection of the life, or of the work,
> And if it take the second must refuse
> A heavenly mansion, raging in the dark.

Even when he seems certain, the lingering doubt remains : (v577)

> 'The work is done,' grown old he thought,
> 'According to my boyish plan;
> Let the fools rage, I swerved in naught,
> Something to perfection brought';
> *But louder sang that ghost, 'What then?'*

If Maud was not in fact that ghost, Yeats certainly had her in mind
when he suggested the paradox with which he lived from 1903 to the
end, and the evidence is clear that he not only understood the political
polarities in his life, but also the importance to his work of the aesthetic

tensions stimulated by these polar extremes. Seen from this angle, Yeats's verse represents the most significant body of political poetry in our time, possibly in all time.

As Yeats reviewed his own career for American audiences in 1932, he suggested that the whole body of his work should be considered a part of the third 'formative movement' of 'the modern Irish nation,' which began, he said, 'almost exactly forty years ago on a stormy autumn morning.' Here as always, almost, Yeats's thoughts about nationalism are also thoughts about Maud. On that stormy morning he had gone to meet Maud at the Dun Laoghaire pier, where they witnessed by accident 'the arrival of Parnell's body.' From the psychic distance of forty years, Yeats looked upon that fabulous day as a symbolic shadowline dividing his earlier work from all that was to follow : 'I have tried to explore, for the sake of my own peace of mind, the origin of what seems to me most unique and strange in our Irish excitement.'[30] 'I collect materials for my thought and work,' he reflected, 'for some identification of my beliefs with the nation itself.'[31] Although Yeats could insist, in 1931, that 'the fall of Parnell had freed imagination from practical politics, from agrarian grievance and political enmity, and turned it to imaginative nationalism, to Gaelic, to the ancient stories, and at last to lyrical poetry and to drama,'[32] he was still aware that 'Man runs his course' 'Between extremities' (v499): 'Hitherto we have walked the road, but now we have shut the door and turned up the lamp.'[33] 'How can they know,' he asked, (v398)

> Truth flourishes where the student's lamp has shone,
> And there alone, that have no solitude?

It is ironic, I think, to compare Yeats's confident assertion that the fall of Parnell had furthered the cause of 'imaginative nationalism' to Kitty O'Shea's equally confident report that Parnell had 'stood appalled at the intensity of the passion of hate that he had loosed, and no one but he – and I with him – knew the awful strength of that

force of destruction.'[34] Yeats knew the awful strength of intellectual
hatred, of course, and was fascinated by it, though he sought (hopefully until 1903) to harness its destructive force. To Maud, in contrast,
Parnell 'had failed when he had repudiated acts of violence,' and she
thought that 'the funeral of the Parliamentary party should have
taken place when [he] was lowered into the grave at Glasnevin'
(174).

Many if not all the good poems of *In the Seven Woods* (1904)
reflect Yeats's agony over the loss of Maud, associated now with this
frustration over cultural integration : (v206–7)

> The old brown thorn-trees break in two high over Cummen Strand,
> Under a bitter black wind that blows from the left hand;
> Our courage breaks like an old tree in a black wind and dies,
> But we have hidden in our hearts the flame out of the eyes
> Of Cathleen, the daughter of Houlihan.

Having given 'all his heart and lost' (v202), Yeats found some
comfort in an old man's wisdom that (v208)

> All that's beautiful drifts away
> Like the waters;

and he sought to (v198)

> put away
> The unavailing outcries and the old bitterness
> That empty the heart.

He had in fact 'forgot awhile' (v198)

> Tara uprooted, and new commonness
> Upon the throne and crying about the streets.

But not for long because he knew 'the folly of being comforted' by rationalisations. Six years later, in his next volume of poems, many of the lyrics reflect the 'reconciliation' Yeats found in the knowledge that 'love is the crooked thing' (v268) and that he 'may wither into the truth' (v261) through the philosophic conclusion that Maud as opposite sets up the tension necessary to creation : (v256)

> Why should I blame her that she filled my days
> With misery, or that she would of late
> Have taught to ignorant men most violent ways,
> Or hurled the little streets upon the great,
> Had they but courage equal to desire?

He recognises frankly that (v256)

> I have come into my strength,
> And words obey my call,

because 'you went from me' (v257).

Several of the lyrics from *The Green Helmet and Other Poems* project a fundamental difference in their approach to social change. To Maud, who was 'half lion, half child,' the answer to land reform was simple : 'Shoot the landlords' (106). This was, to be sure, Maud's solution to all phases of the nationalist problem : 'If ... every Chief Secretary or Lord Lieutenant (or better still, every English king) were shot one after the other,' she wrote, 'Ireland would soon be free with small sacrifice of life' (347). Yeats, of course, was directly opposed to this resolution by fire : (v264)

> How should the world be luckier if this house,
> Where passion and precision have been one
> Time out of mind, became too ruinous
> To breed the lidless eye that loves the sun?

It was, I suppose, to be expected that one who believed in intellectual nationalism should fear the indiscriminate levelling process advocated by the 'other side.' Nothing will be acomplished if (v265)

> The weak lay hand on what the strong has done,
> Till that be tumbled that was lifted high
> And discord follow upon unison,
> And all things at one common level lie.

Some twenty-five years later, in a note to 'Three Songs to the Same Tune,' Yeats was saying the same in even stronger terms : 'In politics I have but one passion and one thought, rancour against all who, except under the most dire necessity, disturb public order, a conviction that public order cannot long persist without the rule of educated and able men. That order was everywhere their work, is still as much a part of their tradition as the *Iliad* or the Republic of Plato; their rule once gone, it lies an empty shell for the passing fool to kick to pieces. Some months ago that passion laid hold upon me with the violence which unfits the poet for all politics but his own. While the mood lasted, it seemed that our growing disorder, the fanaticism that inflamed it like some old bullet imbedded in the flesh, was about to turn our noble history into an ignoble farce'[35] (v543). The refrain from the second of the 'Three Songs,' though referring to an altercation with a neighbour, reflects in its political context Maud's fanatic hatred in contrast to Yeats's passionate conviction that 'Great nations blossom above' : (v547)

> 'Drown all the dogs,' said the fierce young woman,
> 'They killed my goose and a cat.
> Drown, drown in the water-butt,
> Drown all the dogs,' said the fierce young woman.

By this time, ironically, Yeats himself was angry enough to 'Take to the roads and go marching along' because 'nations are empty up there at the top' (v548).

He is no longer as certain as he had been in 1913 when he assured his 'Companions of the Cheshire Cheese' that they had chosen the right way. 'I have kept my faith,' he wrote, then added sadly, (v276)

I am in no good repute
With the loud host before the sea,
That think sword-strokes were better meant
Than lover's music – let that be,
So that the wandering foot's content.

It is clear, of course, that Yeats was not content. Many of the poems of *Responsibilities* almost shout his discontent that 'the blind and ignorant town' (v287) has no 'Delight in Art whose end is peace' (v288). He admits, in a note, that 'we have but a few educated men and the remnants of an old traditional culture among the poor.' Several poems are devoted to a bitter rebuke of 'our new middle class ... showing how base ... at moments of excitement are minds without culture' (v819).

Insisting that 'culture is the sanctity of the intellect,' he filled a diary of these years with 'my discontents,' directed chiefly at 'the lower-middle class' in general and Arthur Griffith in particular: ' ... the political class in Ireland,' he reflected, 'have suffered through the cultivation of hatred as the one energy of their movement, a deprivation which is the intellectual equivalent to a certain surgical operation. Hence the shrillness of their voices. They contemplate all creative power as the eunuchs contemplate Don Juan as he passes through Hell on the white horse.'[36] Although the poems on *The Playboy* and Hugh Lane controversies do not seem to include Maud in their condemnation, Yeats was thinking of her. He implies in several poems of *Responsibilities* that she too is disillusioned: he 'record[s] what's gone,' and comments sadly that (v315)

A crowd
Will gather, and not know it walks the very street
Whereon a thing once walked that seemed a burning cloud.

'She lived in storm and strife' (v317) and will be 'broken in the end' (v313), whereas he, though suffering quite as much, can forgive and find peace through 'companions/ Beyond the fling of the dull ass's hoof,' even though (v321)

... all my priceless things
Are but a post the passing dogs defile.

Between the publication of *Responsibilities* and *The Wild Swans at Coole* (1919) occurred two catastrophes which led Yeats to more profound thoughts on love and war: the Easter Revolution and World War I. Although his initial response to the revolution seems to justify the sacrifice and even suggests it is 'enough/ To know they dreamed and are dead' (v394), many doubts about the ultimate good of armed revolt remain: 'Was it needless death after all?' (v394). The poem to Con Markievicz, who is frequently linked with Maud, suggests sadly that 'too long a sacrifice' has made 'a stone of the heart,' and Yeats recalls (v397)

the years before her mind
Became a bitter, an abstract thing,
Her thought some popular enmity :
Blind and leader of the blind
Drinking the foul ditch where they lie?

And one of the poems to Robert Gregory is bitterly ironic over what 'we called ... a good death' : 'Flit to Kiltartan cross,' he advised the dead Robert, (v791)

```
and stay
Till certain second thoughts have come
Upon the cause you served, that we
Imagined such a fine affair :
Half-drunk or whole-mad soldiery
Are murdering your tenants there.[37]
```

Admitting to himself by 1916 that 'We have no gift to set a states-man right' (v359), Yeats continued to vacillate between nationalistic polarities. One poem, in particular, contrasts his position with Maud's. When he upbraided 'The People' and she 'answered in re-proof,' (v352–3)

```
All I could reply
Was : 'You, that have not lived in thought but deed,
Can have the purity of a natural force,
But I, whose virtues are the definitions
Of the analytic mind, can neither close
The eye of the mind nor keep my tongue from speech '
```

So it was to the very end : 'The poet stubborn with his passion' (v356) sang the 'victories of the mind' but 'dream[ed] of a Ledaean body,' frequently managing to suggest in the mind-body dilemma the para-dox of Ireland's nationalistic struggle.[38] Although he wanted to believe 'there are men who have made their art/ Out of no tragic war' (v369), Yeats was not one of these. He felt that he (v384)

```
had been undone
By Homer's Paragon
Who never gave the burning town a thought;
```

and he hoped that (v385)

```
She would have time to turn her eyes,
... upon the glass
And on the instant would grow wise.
```

He never ceased to imagine what might have happened to him and Maud, and to Ireland by extension, if they had been able to avoid the (v506)

> Great hatred, little room, [which]
> Maimed us at the start.

'To be choked with hate,' he wrote in 'A Prayer for My Daughter,' 'May well be of all evil chances chief.' He expanded this observation with a distinction in kinds of hatred which he increasingly emphasised in his late years : (v405)

> An intellectual hatred is the worst,
> So let her think opinions are accursed.
> Have I not seen the loveliest woman born
> Out of the mouth of Plenty's horn,
> Because of her opinionated mind
> Barter that horn and every good
> By quiet natures understood
> For an old bellows full of angry wind?

In order to justify his own impassioned reaction to social and political affairs, Yeats associated the 'arrogance and hatred' of Maud and Con with 'the wares/Peddled in the thoroughfares' (v406), in contrast to 'the spiritual intellect's great work' (v632). It was the 'abstract hatred' of 'soldier, assassin, executioner' (v482) in contrast to the concrete wrath of the artist. There were, of course, times during 'The Troubles' when Yeats himself, his (v426)

> wits astray
> Because of all that senseless tumult, all but cried
> For vengeance on the murderers of Jacques Molay.

Realising that he was about to fall into the trap he had warned against so diligently, he explained in a note: 'A cry for vengeance because of the murder of the Grand Master of the Templars seems to me fit symbol for those who labour for hatred, and so for sterility in various kinds' (v827). It 'fed class hatred,' the very development he sought to counteract in the Unity of Culture.

Yeats knew from observation, however, that the passion of politics might be unifying, and he had learned from William Blake that 'the tygers of wrath are wiser than the horses of instruction.' But Blake's 'honest indignation' is one thing, 'abstract hatred' another. If Yeats was to avoid 'the logic of fanaticism' (v837), he needed to assume the mask of (v576)

> Timon and Lear
> Or that William Blake
> Who beat upon the wall
> Till Truth obeyed his call.

Or, of course, Jonathan Swift, to whom he was indebted for (v481)

> *Saeva indignatio* and the labourer's hire,
> The strength that gives our blood and state magnanimity of its own desire;
> Everything that is not God consumed with intellectual fire.

Tempted perhaps but not fierce enough to mount Maud's wagonette, Yeats nevertheless studied 'hatred with great diligence,' (v558)

> For that's a passion in my own control,
> A sort of besom that can clear the soul
> Of everything that is not mind or sense.

From this conclusion emerges the teasing paradox that 'Hatred of

God may bring the soul to God' (v558), which lies at the heart of Yeats's dilemma. As the artist (v637)

> lives and dies
> Between his two eternities,
> That of race and that of soul,

he realises that the intellectual tension necessary to the creation of 'a rest for the people of God' demands the union of contraries: Davis and Mitchel, Pearse and Connolly, Eva Gore-Booth and Constance, W. B. and Maud. 'Under Ben Bulben' is convincing evidence that these nationalistic polarities were urgent to the very end: (v638)

> You that Mitchel's prayer have heard,
> 'Send war in our time, O Lord!'
> Know that when all words are said
> And a man is fighting mad,
> Something drops from eyes long blind,
> He completes his partial mind,
> For an instant stands at ease,
> Laughs aloud, his heart at peace.
> Even the wisest man grows tense
> With some sort of violence
> Before he can accomplish fate,
> Know his work or choose his mate.

And it may well be that some degree of intellectual hatred is a necessary complement to any satisfactory scheme of intellectual nationalism. Cathleen ni Houlihan could be 'Mother Ireland with the Crown of Stars about her head,'[39] but as Sean O'Casey observed on a riotous night at the Abbey, 'one who had the walk of a queen could be a bitch at times.'[40]

Two lectures on the Irish theatre by W. B. Yeats

ROBERT O'DRISCOLL

We had originally intended to publish in this volume three lectures on the Irish theatre which Yeats delivered during his American tour in 1903–4. Copies of these lectures were discovered by Professor Richard Londraville (State University of New York, Potsdam) in the home of Mrs Jeanne Robert Foster, a friend of Yeats and John Quinn, and one-time editor of *The Review of Reviews* and the *Transatlantic Review*. Senator Michael Yeats, however, had the originals of these and other lectures his father delivered on his American tour, a list of the places where the lectures were given, and also detailed 'directions' which Quinn had compiled to make the trip less wearisome. The directors of the Cuala Press, therefore, decided not to break up the material, and all of it will be released as a Cuala Press volume in a year or two.

Senator Yeats, however, generously provided two substitute manuscripts. The first, a typescript of a lecture to be delivered during Yeats's American tour in 1914, was delivered on 19 December 1913 in the home of a Mrs Fowler, but apart from the fact that she lived at 26 Gilbert Street, Oxford Street W., London, I am unable to provide further information about her relationship with Yeats. The second manuscript was that of a paper which Yeats sent to be read at 'a Cali-

fornian School,' San José, where he had lectured in January 1904.[1]
I discovered, however, that the second manuscript was published in
1924 in *The Voice of Ireland (Glōr na h-Ēireann) A Survey of the
Race and Nation from all Angles, by the foremost leaders at home and
abroad* (Dublin, Manchester, London, and Blackburn: John Hey-
wood), edited by William G. Fitz-gerald, but as the paper has not
been reprinted, and as the material is relevant to the subject of our
book, we have reprinted it here.

The manuscript of the first lecture is a seventeen-page typescript
with deletions, corrections, and insertions by Yeats in ink. I have included in the notes all significant material that has been altered. At
various points in the manuscript there are marks of omission and as
these presumably were places where Yeats intended to speak extempore
I have included them in the transcript. I have regularised spelling,
expanded abbreviations, inserted apostrophes, completed quotation
marks, supplied terminal punctuation, and completed the punctuation of parenthetical phrases.

The manuscript of the second paper, a twenty-four page Yeats
holograph which has been torn from an exercise book, is in an ex-
tremely rough state; there are many deletions and substitutions. The
chief difference between the manuscript and printed text is that the
manuscript version has ten sections, while the printed version has
only two sections. The punctuation and syntax have been improved
in the printed version, and as it is likely that Yeats corrected the proofs
I have followed the printed version. I have included in the notes all
significant variations between the manuscript and printed versions
of the paper.

*Lecture by Mr W. B. Yeats given at the house of Mrs Fowler,
26 Gilbert Street, Oxford Street W. on Friday, 19th December, 1913,
at 3.15.*

I asked Mrs Fowler to invite you to hear me speak today and I want to explain to you what I explained yesterday to my audience. I am going to lecture in America. I am going to lecture in the American Universities and Societies as that is the only way of getting at my own countrymen. I have had to get at them in Ireland through the English Press. I have to get at them in America largely through the Universities and their literary organisations. Our own Press is very unintelligent. It acts on the simple plan of publishing you if it agrees and not if it does not. The result is that our own Press never changes its mind, and we have no system of lecturing of an efficient kind. I therefore asked two friends to get audiences of their friends, and I want you to question me if there is anything you do not understand, because if you do not understand a thing I will have to explain in my lecture and make it clear.

What I want [is] to try and give some definition of what bad dramatic literature is, and try to find some definition of good dramatic literature. I am going to describe some little part of the history of my own theatre which will be touring in America whilst I am lecturing there.

The ordinary theatre as we have it today, the theatre which is a vast vested interest making a great deal of money for a great many people, the commercial theatre – well that makes a great deal of money precisely because it is not literature. If you analyse any popular play which draws great multitudes, you will find it essentially topical. I mean by that when the various characters come on to the stage you know at once what they are by their make-up. You have met them before. You have seen something almost exactly the same in a great number of plays, and the play is an immense success if it manages to touch in your heart some piece of purely topical sentiment. And the proof that it is purely topical is that twenty years later hearing that play is revived you go to see it thinking you will have your old enchantment, instead of which you feel how very old-fashioned it is. And this group of topical interests it appeals to are largely a group of moral interests – often a damnable system of morals, but one you think you believe in, but fortunately for the world you seldom act on it. I remember seeing *Mice and Men*[2] some years ago and I remember the central event of that play – the hero has a mistress, a married woman. In time he goes abroad and when after some years he comes back in a fit of moral enthusiasm he decides to marry a young girl. His mistress, who is represented as waiting for him in faithful love, writes a letter of welcome, but he throws it into the dirty clothes basket where it is found by the husband. ... [3] The whole theatre applauded, and no doubt any man in the theatre would have blackballed that man in his club, but in the theatre he applauded, because we do not go to the theatre to have our understanding and charity enlarged. But of course ten years later he might be touched by a different group of moral interests, and then he would be shocked.

That is the commercial play, novel, pamphlet, etc. It is the appeal to a group of emotions which for some reason or other are fashionable, and you will find that every theatrical manager will say that it is impossible to tell what is going to be successful – that is because they are not sure if they have the fashionable ingredient for their pudding. A man who knows his business knows what is a good play, but nobody knows what is topical, what touches the fashionable interest.

There is another form of topical interest, and that is the humanitarian play that touches our political and social instincts. I have the greatest respect for those who write it. I admire them immensely. ... A play like Mr Galsworthy's *Justice*[4] appeals to a topical interest of the educated. It appeals to certain feelings that have been aroused in us by the papers. It appeals to us to reform the prisons. We come away greatly interested. If we go back without that particular topical interest we discover how dull it is. For there is nothing of human life there. In order to make his study of institutions[5] he has had to take types who are hardly human beings at all. A barrister is merely a barrister, a clerk is merely a clerk, and in the end you discover that the victim is merely a victim. He is purely a traditional character who exists in the world of imagination to suffer the wrongs the humani-

tarians heap upon him. The scene which made the greatest sensation
was when the victim in the dark beat upon the door. Prisoners beat on
their cell doors when they are bored,[6] and in the play someone begins
to beat upon the door and you hear far away someone else beating on
his door and the prisoner at last can bear it no more and does the
same, and the audience was carried away by enthusiasm, but I can
assure you anyone can beat upon a door in the dark. We all felt our
humanitarian principles excited. ... It is literature from which human
life has been eliminated in the interests of a topical interest. ...

In great realistic art a piece of life is so completely expressed that
it is put outside the changes of fashion. Take a novel of Flaubert –
everything, no fluctuation of time can ever affect it. ... Everything
is there and because of this complete exposition of a great work of art
it is dull always to the idle, it is dull to those who are not ready to
come with[7] the passion to understand, and so no great work of art can
for a moment compete with the temporary works which appeal to the
topical interest, and because they do teach you nothing and give you no
labour they merely express what you feel already. But this complete
exposition of a group of circumstances and characters is great realistic
art. I remember once questioning some neighbours of mine who were
bored by Stevenson. I questioned them to find out why Stevenson
bored them, and it was because it was [of] the description of characters and of scenes. In other words, because he was making his exposition of a piece of life complete. ...

There is another kind of exposition – or perhaps expression is better
than exposition – and that is where you completely express not the
outer but the inner life, the life of our emotions. There is one fundamental difference between the exposition of the inner life and any
group of external circumstances. If I need the most complete external
exposition of any man's life I cannot give him a greater memory than
is in that life, I cannot begin before his birth. The things he talks of
will be what he has heard of during say the seventy years of his life.
But if I give an exposition of my own mind, I am the spectator of the

ages. The Tale of Troy is quite near to me, probably much nearer than anything I read in this morning's paper; or, on the other hand, if my turn is for biblical mythology, Judea is nearer than the Balkans, but I do not talk of them. They do not enter into my business life. In external circumstances I keep to the speech in which people ordinarily talk, but when I am going to express my own mind, the things I think of when alone, the things I feel as a solitary man – then I want all culture. I cannot know too much. I want a vast symbolism, a phantasmagoria going back to the beginning of the world, and always the Tale of Troy, of Judea, will be nearer to me than my own garden, because I am not limited by time. I am as old as mankind. Out of all that rises the inner art of poetry, the language of music and the arts, which is not the natural language. You can expound outer circumstances through natural speech, through the speech which has been created through ordinary instincts of men living their lives, but the moment you begin to expound these things which can hardly be expounded in words you need this artificial, inner language which is passed on from age to age, often not consisting of words that convey an idea, but merely of sounds ... simply because in my soul I am the spectator of the ages, and you can only create great emotional literature by bringing back a great traditional culture, and in emotional literature the greater the work of art the more clearly it shows its ancestry. In realistic literature the greater the work of art the more it hides its ancestry, because it has to do with a group of people who never lived before and never will again, but in a great emotional work of art there must be no conscious originality,[8] only the mark of its high breeding, its eternal descent.

Virgil walks with Dante through the three worlds because he (Dante) wishes to proclaim the descent of his art from Virgil, just as Virgil proclaimed his from Homer, and as Milton proclaimed his from Virgil and many predecessors. There is no self-conscious originality.

... You who live in towns go to books at need. We in Ireland went to the ancient literature of the common people and it was the history of that literature in Ireland which gave Lady Gregory and Synge and myself the hope of creating there a permanent literature. Because this learned artificial language was created by and is associated with permanent minds, it has nothing to do with passing fashions which I have described as affecting a theatre audience. It descends to us from minds who have proved themselves permanent – above fashion. In the same way the peasant has his great literature, descending from men who spoke or sang their poems and did not write them.

I remember once being at a picnic in Ireland, and feeling very bored I had wandered away by myself, and I came across two old shepherds with whom I got into conversation for I thought they would be interested in permanent human life. So I began to question them about the surroundings, and I mentioned a certain great house of the neighbourhood and asked them if they remembered who lived there. 'Oh yes,' said one of them, 'that is where Colonel Martin lived. He was in my father's time.' And then they began, first one and then the other telling a bit of the story: 'Colonel Martin was a great traveller who went all over the world who knew all languages, the Russ, the Pruss, and the Span, and when he was away his wife thought she would never see him again and so, saving your presence, she took up with a rich man. She took up with a rich man in Galway, and when Colonel Martin came back he knew his wife was there in the big house with the rich man, but he had no evidence. So he changed clothes with a pedlar and went with the most beautiful jewellery and went and showed it to the servant, and said "Let your mistress take what she likes," and the servant took the pack and went away with it and he followed, and she went on, opening door after door (notice the peasant mind excited by the idea of door after door). He followed, but she did not hear because he had slippers on, and presently she went inside the door and he heard his wife say "That is the step of Colonel Martin," and through the door he saw her in bed with the rich man. He rushed in and saw a pistol which he pointed at the rich man in the bed with his wife and then he stopped and said he would not shoot as he was defenceless, so he walked out, but he had his evidence and got his case, for which he got two kegs of gold, and when he had the gold he scattered it in the streets ...'

There is an imagination which created perfectly normal circumstances, and I have got a great many stories from the people in Ireland. They always remember a man for something he was in himself, not for anything he has done for them. Colonel Martin because he was an absorbing personality in himself is remembered today. That is the spirit which creates great literature. I found that a village poet wrote about a certain Helen[9] who was remembered as was Helen of Troy, and I went to the cottages for stories about her, and one old woman said: 'I tremble all over when I think of her.' Another said: 'The sun and moon never shone upon anything so lovely.' And this great fame has come to her because of the song that was made about her by a wandering poet. He lived in the early decades of last century.

This imagination of the people has been kept alive by their traditional literature, the heroic literature of Ireland. Lady Gregory has translated a great deal of it in a book I put beside the *Morte d'Arthur*. She has put it into the language of the people. ... One of the most beautiful is that of Oisin and St Patrick,[10] of all stories the most popular is the Argument between Oisin and St Patrick.

Oisin had gone into fairyland and lived there for years with a fairy mistress, and then one day he asks if he may go back to Ireland. She consents, but says that he must not alight from his horse. ... And so he went, but seeing two men staggering under a heavy burden and attempting to stoop from his horse to lift the burden from them, his saddle girth broke and he touched the ground, and he at once became 300 years old ... he was brought to the convent of St Patrick where he lived complaining of Christianity. His arguments with St Patrick provide an old drama which is known in every Irish-speaking cottage in Ireland. ... Patrick has told him that Finn his father is in hell ... and for centuries that last cry of paganism has gone on in the cottages, has been repeated by grandfathers to their grandchildren ... 'I will cry but not for God, but because Finn and the Fianna are not living!'

Our first thought was to take this old literature and to put it into verse plays, into ordinary English. But it was only gradually that we came to understand that finer than the literature itself was the wonderful speech of the people. When you get away from crowds, when you get to lonely men, their speech itself is a work of art. When you analyse any material, the stage, anything you like, and begin to make it as emotionally expressive as possible, you will always find that it gets less and less capable of expressing fact.[11] Now this speech of the country people of Ireland is not efficient for expressing facts. You could not carry on the speech of the towns in this leisured Galway speech. It is full of extravagant images, the people using it caress their words, they delight in them, they prolong beautiful words, and we discovered that this speech was the most powerful instrument we could have in literature. It enabled us to keep fairly close to reality and yet use that old culture, to put plays upon the stage which have much of the quality of poetical[12] drama ... where the unprinted culture has drifted into the ordinary life of the people. One writer of my school is so convinced that you could put anything in the world into it that he translated certain of Petrarch's sonnets,[13] the most artificial literature in the world, essentially of that artificial learned speech of the poets, and yet it goes without a change into this typical speech of the unlettered, whose culture is quite as ancient as that of the learned. I will read two of Petrarch's sonnets written in Irish dialect, i.e., the dialect of these people. ... They think in Gaelic but they speak in English.

(reads sonnets)

And then there is another which I think one of the most extraordinarily poignant things in literature, and I will read it.

(reads sonnet)

We had dreams of representing in Ireland what has been done in Swiss Italy, and in Sicily by Grasso[14] ... that is very much what we tried to do, but when we brought our art to Dublin we had an extraordinary battle before us. We had the same fight as is going on here between men who are trying to write plays of permanent literature for the theatre against the topical – here[15] it is Humanitarian theatre – in Ireland the political ... topical drama like *Mice and Men* ... in Ireland created by the accidental bourgeoisie of the priests.[16] Then we had to fight a theatre of politics that no longer represented great patriots like Emmet ... this theatre had no existence until we began, but the moment we commenced to make a theatre these points of view became at once apparent. Dramatists[17] rose up who wanted their politicians as pure as possible. Instead of Mr Galsworthy's Judge,[18] you had England the eternal enemy, and whenever we put on a spirited piece of life in which Ireland refused to take the part of the victim,[19] everyone was furious. If we put on one who was not virtuous that interfered greatly ... the great object of the religious was to keep everything rose-pink, a state where everybody could be kept in perfect ignorance till the age of 30 when they admitted that a little knowledge of the world was inevitable. ...

We took the old Irish peasant Grania, we modified her ... we made her a very much quieter person than she was in the legend and put her on the stage. There was a great outcry at once. Then again I put on Cuchulain who killed his father[20] and they were most indignant that I took this discreditable incident to write about. ... I did not think we could have had a victory such as came to Scotland with Burns. ... When Scotland thought itself very pious and entirely occupied with the world to come, there came Burns. ... Taine believed that the man of genius always expressed his environment, but instead of that came Burns expressing his great satisfaction in drink and devilry generally.

In Ireland the great idea was to keep these set attitudes ... this arrangement of human nature, that it could never do anything unexpected, that would never upset carefully calculated propaganda.[21] Into this came a mind incapable of politics, incapable of any idea about which people could found a society – the mind of John Synge. I met him in Paris in 1877.[22] He had been wandering all over Europe carrying his fiddle with him, and this opened all hearts to him. He did not live by his fiddle but simply carried it about with him probably playing it in return for stories from the peasants whom he met in his wanderings. He had £40 a year, and with the addition of a suit of clothes given him by relations he managed to live a contented life for ten years, during which he had gone in perpetual pursuit of the poor. He had no humanitarian interest in the poor, he was just a kind and friendly person. He never thought of the man he walked with on the highroad as a poor man. He liked them because he thought they were picturesque, because they had before their minds the simple, normal facts of life.

I urged him to come to Ireland and he went to the Aran Islands and Galway and then on to the Blasket Islands, which are so primitive that the head of the Island is called the 'king,' and Synge used to stay with the king. They never paid taxes for 40 years ... they drowned the taxgatherer. They talk quite openly about it – it is evidently the one joyous moment of their lives. Synge used to go there where he got deep into the folk life, and he came to Dublin full of these thoughts, all of which upset the nice little row of china figures put upon the wall. ...

When we get an educated Ireland, not timid, not caring in fact whether its character is slandered or not, we shall have them with us, but we have the other Ireland who would prefer to give up any truth if it could remove from itself a little alarm, who would give up the salvation of its soul if it could be sure no one would slander it. The 'Playboy's' love of mischief[23] which must have been instinctive in the depths of Synge's soul affronted the row of china figures. ...

When I went to Aran I went in a fishing boat. It was a misty day and I suppose my arrival was rather mysterious. ... One of the fishermen said to me : 'We will bring you to the oldest man in the Island' ... and he said 'if there is any gentleman has done a crime we will hide him. There was a gentleman that killed his father and I hid him in my house six months until he got away to America' – it was evidently the most joyous moment of his life. We all love criminals – all of us in our hearts love such a man. We may think him dangerous, but as a criminal simply he has our entire sympathy – he is at any rate an audacious person who had not been tamed. The old man knew quite well he was saying : 'I am not tamed, I may be 80, but I am not tamed.' And Synge took all this tameless thought and put it into his play.

The Playboy arrives at a little shebeen where Pegeen the daughter of the publican is sitting. After some talk he confesses that he has killed his father and though at first he has no pride in the deed, feeling the evident delight in his recital and the sympathy extended to him, he begins to think he has done a fine thing. And that is exactly the feeling he would arouse in the Island. The idea is that for a man to have killed his father, he must have had great provocation. ... He has hit the law between the eyes, he has hit decency in the eyes – I wonder why he did it, they ask. The Playboy then begins to explain that his father was quite impossible and they agree with him. As he proceeds his tale becomes more and more heroic, and the girls treat him as a hero, bringing butter, food, etc. In the midst of these recitals his father himself turns up and the people are so scornful of the Playboy that his idea is to make amends by really killing his father. But when he actually begins to do it under their eyes then the ordinary law-abiding man begins to emerge.

This play is the natural instinct of everyone all over the world – to love the spirited man, to love courage and hate timidity.

I have said enough, I think, to show what Ireland has been with its set ideas ... their newspapers are a disgrace, everyone despises our Press. They have been left alone to get into these set ideas on every question. So just as Burns came to Scotland with his glorification of drink, so came Synge to Ireland with his assertion of the capricious mind. The mind that will say always the thing that you do not want to have said. Freedom symbolised, and moving in front of you like an Angel of Freedom.

Our members at first were members of a little Coffee Palace, whom we were able to train from the beginning. When they were not at work they were members of a society with all the old set doubts. One of the members said to Synge he thought they would have a great success with a play on the Tale of the Rebellion of '98. The result was a play in which a quarrel is taking place between a Protestant and a Catholic woman, one abusing the Pope and the other Queen Elizabeth. One feared the soldiers and the other the rebels ... in the end one goes away, preferring to meet any fate rather than stay longer in the company of the other. The play, however, was not received with enthusiasm and so it was never completed.

I said in my lecture yesterday[24] that all great literature is a battle. Tragic literature, as I see it, is battle in the depth of a man's soul. He feels the lack of something and he creates, as Dante did, the vision of divine justice. Beatrice dies, and he creates a vision of divine love. It would take me too long to give proof that the ecstasy of tragic art differs from happiness,[25] because it can only exist with pain ... whereas ecstasy is got when the intellect has shown you the whole vision of reality and you have brought your imagination to peace by bringing something from the invisible world, the compensating dream ... you have completed the picture so that your imagination is at peace. Realism is a battle in the outer world; it is the contest of two realities, and we have come to realise that Ireland is in the midst of that contest. Out of that battle is coming our art, and it is because of the stupidity of our opponents. ... The battle that began with Synge is going on for generations, and there is growing up among the young a passionate hatred of that row of china figures. They are beginning to break them one by one and as they continue our Press becomes more and more indignant. We have to bring together in Ireland the remnants of that old folk faith, giving us a beautiful romantic literature if we see it rightly. ... Then we can create a great imaginative poetical literature for the internal and external battle.

At present we are getting a very sound, realistic literature from our young men who are carrying on the work of Synge, but he was no mere realist. In his comedies there is the eternal battle – he is a tragi-comedian. ... The tragedian finds that something in his own soul – the comedian finds it in the world. All comedy is satire. Satire is essentially battle.

THE IRISH DRAMATIC MOVEMENT

A Letter to the Students of a Californian School by W. B. Yeats[26]

THE PRELUDE

Twenty years ago I was entertained at dinner by certain monks or friars in a Californian village that I forget the name of. I was to lecture to their students, who were all of Irish descent, and as I walked to the hall under the moonlight, through a quadrangle full of palm-trees, I felt some anxiety. I had been given home-brewed wine, and thinking it as harmless as the raisin-wine or ginger-wine of Ireland or England, had drunk incautiously, and it had gone to my head. I felt slightly stupid, and wondered if it would spoil the lecture; but I had not spoken for five minutes before I felt at my ease.

I quoted some fragment of Young Ireland poetry, and there was just that immediate applause that would have welcomed it at home. As I went on speaking I felt that those lads, not one of whom had, it may be, seen Ireland, did not differ from Dublin lads of the same age in imagination or in literary knowledge. It pleases me to think that school has changed in nothing, except that it is no longer permitted to brew its own wine; and I will therefore – being a little chilled by the vast audience our editor has promised me – address my letter to its students. I will suppose that my letter is to be read out, and that all students under fifteen years of age will be sent to bed before the reading begins, and that those who remain know the Ireland of history, while they are ignorant of modern Ireland.

THE LETTER

Some twenty-four years ago, Lady Gregory, who was near her fiftieth year, and I, who was in my early thirties, planned the foundation of an Irish Theatre, and we were soon joined by John Synge, who was in his late twenties. Lady Gregory had spent most of her life between two great houses in South Galway, while Synge had wandered over half Europe with his fiddle, and I had gone to and fro between Dublin and London. Yet Synge and I – like Lady Gregory – were people of the country; I because of my childhood and youth in Sligo, and he because of his in Wicklow. We had gone, all three, from cottage to cottage, collecting stories and hearing songs, and we thought that in these we had discovered that portion of the living mind of Ireland that was most beautiful and distinguished, and we wished to bring what we had discovered to Dublin, where, it seemed to us, the popular mind had grown harsh and ugly. We did not think that the Irish country lacked vice; we were even to be denounced because we insisted that they had the brutalities of country people elsewhere; but we were certain of the beauty of the songs and stories.

Lady Gregory had taken down a song in Irish – 'The Grief of a Girl's Heart' it is called – and one day she showed it to a Gaelic-speaking man at her door, and asked what were the best verses. He picked just those verses that I would have picked – those that are most wild and strange, most unlike anything that is called 'popular poetry':

My heart is black as the blackness of the sloe, or as the coal that is left on the smith's forge; or as the sole of a shoe left in white halls; it was you put that darkness over my life.

You have taken the East from me; you have taken the West from me; you have taken what is before me and what is behind me. You have taken the moon, you have taken the sun from me; and my fear is great that you have taken God from me !

Amid your semi-tropical scenery, you think of Ireland as a far-off country of romance, and you will find it hard to understand one very prosaic reality.[27] If a man is creating some new thing he has to question the taste of others, and that makes those others angry, and all the more if that new thing is a part of something they have long looked down upon as ignorant or foolish or old-fashioned. Then, too, even if he does not openly question the taste of others, it will be a long time before they can see the beauty that he has seen. I think it was George Henry Lewes who said that at first he could see no merit in the Elgin Marbles; and I remember an essay by Andrew Lang, in which he apologised for some attack on the poetry of my generation by saying that when he first met with the poetry of that very great poet, Paul Veraine, he thought it no better than the rhymes in some country newspaper. George Henry Lewes and Andrew Lang had much taste and great erudition. We had to convince average men and women, and to do this by an art that must blunder and experiment that it might find some new form.

If any of you become artists or poets, do not ask a welcome from great crowds, but write at first for a few friends, and always for a comparatively few people – not because you scorn the crowd, but because you think so well of it that you will offer it nothing but your best. In a few generations – but a short time in the history of a masterpiece – that crowd will speak of you with respect, if you are a great artist or poet, and a sufficient number will study what you have made with pleasure and profit.[28]

We thought that Irish drama would be historical or legendary, and in verse or romantic prose; neither Synge nor Lady Gregory had written plays, nor had indeed thought of doing so; so it was I – my head full of poetical drama – that gave the theatre its first impulse. After an experiment with English actors, we began our real work in 1902 in a little temperance hall in a back street, and chose our players from boys and girls, whose interests were, with a couple of exceptions, more political than literary. For the next two or three years we moved from hall to hall making some reputation among students of literature, and among young patriots who thought a theatre with Irish plays might strengthen national feeling, but [we were] much derided by the newspapers. One night I came in front of the curtain and asked the audience to support us against our enemies. I quoted from a leading article in one of the morning newspapers, which had said: 'Mr Yeats proposes to perform foreign masterpieces' – that was part of our project at the time – 'Foreign masterpieces are very dangerous things.' I was angry; I should, perhaps, have remembered that the Elgin Marbles are 'foreign masterpieces,' and that some of the figures are very unclothed. Among my audience was an English friend, Miss Horniman. I had been hoping – she had made one or two hints – that she would give us a subscription, and as she was rich, I had fixed upon twenty pounds as the amount. She came up to me the moment I had finished, and said: 'I will buy or build you a theatre.' In the next few months she bought and rebuilt a little old theatre that had been part of a Mechanics' Institute, and we opened there in the winter of 1903–4.

Our obscurity made it possible to create a new kind of acting, for it gave us time to prepare and experiment. If our players had been stage-struck young men and women of the usual kind, they would have developed much more quickly; but their art would have been the ordinary stage art of their time. I had once been asked, at the end of a lecture, where we would get our players, for at that time there were neither Irish players nor Irish plays. I answered with the first thing that came into my head: 'I will go into a room where there are a lot of people, and write all the names on slips of paper and drop them into a hat, shake them up, and take out twelve slips. I will ask those twelve people to act our plays.'

Certainly William Fay, an electric light fitter, who was also an actor of genius, had some experience, for he had toured Ireland in a company with a Negro actor-manager; and his brother, Frank Fay, was learned in the history of the stage, and fond of reciting poetry. But our women players were almost chosen at hazard. They all belonged to a political association, 'The Daughters of Erin,' that described itself as educating the children of the poor, but was described by its enemies as teaching a catechism that began with the question: 'What is the origin of evil?' and the answer was – 'England!' From this Association we got two actresses of genius – Miss Sara Allgood, and Miss Moira O'Neill. They grew but slowly to skill and power because, acting at first more from patriotism than ambition, they were never tempted to copy some popular favourite. They copied, under the guidance of William Fay, the life they had seen in their own homes, or saw during some country visit; or they searched, under the guidance of Frank Fay or of myself, for some traditional measured speech to express those emotions that we feel, but cannot observe.

I soon saw that their greatest success would be in comedy, or in observed tragedy; not in poetical drama, which needs considerable poetical and general culture. I had found an old Dublin pamphlet about the blind beggar, 'Zozimus,'[29] and noticed that whereas the parts written in ordinary English are badly written, certain long passages in dialect are terse and vivid. I pointed this out to Lady Gregory, and said if we could persuade our writers to use dialect, no longer able to copy the newspapers, or some second-rate English author, they would become original and vigorous. Perhaps no one reason ever drives one to anything. Perhaps I do not remember clearly after so many years; but I believe it was that thought that made me write, with Lady Gregory's help, *The Pot of Broth,* and *Cathleen ni Houlihan.* The dialect in those two plays is neither rich nor supple, for I had not the right ear, and Lady Gregory had not as yet taken down among the cottages two hundred thousand words of folklore. But they began the long series of plays in dialect that have given our theatre the greater portion of its fame.

I once said to John Synge, 'Why is it that an early Renaissance building[30] is so much more beautiful than anything that followed?' And he replied, 'Style is from the shock of new material.' It was the shock of new material that gave our plays and players their admirable style. I insist on the word 'style.' When I saw Miss O'Neill play the old drunken woman in *The Tinker's Wedding*, at the Birmingham Repertory Theatre a few years ago, I thought her performance incredibly distinguished – nothing second-hand, nothing from the common stock of the stage; no *cliché*, no recognition of all that traditional humour about drunken women.[31]

Lady Gregory's little farces are the only farces of modern times that have not only humour but beauty of style; and her tragedy, *The Gaol Gate*, is a classic, and not because of its action, for it has no action, but because of its style. One need not commend the style of John Synge's famous plays – *The Well of the Saints*, or *The Playboy, The Riders to the Sea, Deirdre of the Sorrows*. Should our Abbey Theatre come to an end, should our plays cease to be acted, we shall be remembered, I think, because we were the first to give to the English-speaking Ireland a mastery of style by turning a dialect that had been used hitherto with a comic purpose to a purpose of beauty. If I were your professor of literature (I must remind myself that *you* hear me, while others but overhear) and were compelled to choose examples of fine prose for an Irish reading book, I would take some passages from Swift, some from Burke,[32] one perhaps from Mitchel (unless his mimicry of Carlyle should put me off), and from that on find no comparable passages till *The Gaol Gate* and the last act of *Deirdre of the Sorrows*. I would then set my pupils to show that this strange English, born in the country cottages, is a true speech with as old a history as the English of Shakespeare, and that it takes its vocabulary from Tudor England and its construction from the Gaelic.

The dialect drama in the hands of Mr Fitzmaurice, Mr T. C.

Murray, Mr Lennox Robinson, Mr Boyle, Mr Daniel Corkery, and
Mr Seumas O'Kelly, and of Mr Padraic Colum in one of his plays,
took a new turn. Synge and Lady Gregory were as little interested in
social questions as the old men and women whose stories they had
heard and copied; but our new dramatists were, in imagination and
sympathy, mainly of the city. The countryman is much alone, and if,
as happened through all the Middle Ages, when the most beautiful
of our stories were invented, he is of a violent and passionate nature,
he seeks relief from himself in stories or in songs full of delicate emotion : he delights, perhaps, in Arthur and his Court. In the cities, however, men who are in continual contact with one another have for their
first need not the beauty but, as I think, the truth of human life. They
suffer much from irritation, anger, jealousy; and in their hearts they
desire to be shown that, though capitalist and labourer, Nationalist
and Unionist, Republican and Free Stater, even honest men and
bribed, differ in one thing, they are alike in a hundred. They wish to
see themselves and the enemy of their working hours explained, derided or bantered, with at least occasional good humour, though they
are not philosophic enough to know that art is the chief intellectual
form of charity. When some play of this kind is acted, they are startled,
sometimes angry, sometimes incredulous; but they are not bored. They
cannot be shown too many such plays if we are not to murder or be
murdered because we have given or received some partisan name.
Such plays, in the hands of the writers I have named, have dealt with
the life of the shop and workshop, and of the well-off farmer, more
often than of those small farms of Connaught where there is so much
folklore; and the scene is laid, as a general rule, in or near some considerable town, and their speech comes close to modern English.
Except in the plays of Mr Lennox Robinson, however, where some
character is introduced whose speech has no admixture of dialect,
characterisation becomes conventional and dialogue stilted. They introduce such characters so often that I wonder at times if the dialect
drama has not exhausted itself – if most of those things have not been

said that our generation wants to have said in that particular form. Perhaps, having created certain classics, the dramatic genius of Ireland will pass on to something else.

What new form shall we invent? Or shall we but find new material, and so give the old form new interest? Perhaps on the whole it is likely that we shall but find new material. Ireland is full of tragedy and ruin; and though at the moment we have to reject the few new plays that deal with it, because they are full of the distortion of party feeling, that phase will pass. In a year or two there will be personal narratives, separate incidents which detach themselves. Motives will become apparent; we shall be able to see it all separated from our own fears and hopes, as if upon the luminous table of a *camera obscura*. We have to make peace among so many passions that are the most violent Ireland has known in modern days – violent not only because there has been so much suffering, but because great intellectual questions are involved.

When should we distinguish between political and private morality, or is there only one morality? What is the part of the Catholic Church in public life? How far must the State respect humanitarian emotion? As all these things have been fought out in country districts, or, if in towns, by those classes which still use a language that has in some degree what is called 'dialect' – that is to say, elements peculiar to Ireland – I have a little hope that I shall not be compelled, as one of the readers for the Abbey Theatre, to read through a great number of plays in ordinary English, where all is bookish and pedantic, or full of humorous or sentimental *clichés*.

Yet perhaps my first thought is correct, and that we are about to create a new form, and that this form will deal more with those classes who have lost almost every distinctive Irish form of speech. The other day a strange Irish novel was published – *Ulysses*, by Mr James Joyce – which is certainly a new form. You are too young to read it – your master would rightly take it from you. It would cost you some pounds to buy a copy, and if you bought it you would be too startled by its incredible coarseness to see its profundity.

Every other successful Irish novel – certainly every other whose name I can recall at the moment – resembles our plays in dealing with some simple story of public or private life by the light of a morality which everyone accepts without hesitation. Great works of art have been written in that way – the comedies of Oliver Goldsmith, and nearly all the comedies of Molière, for instance. But there are other works which are also, as a famous Belgian poet said a masterpiece must be, a portion of the conscience of mankind, and which judge all by the light of some moral discovery.[33] Something which has been there always – more constantly there, indeed, than Tony Lumpkins or the miser – but which has not been noticed, is brought out into the light that we may perceive [that] it is beautiful or good, or most probably that it is evil or ugly. The plays of Strindberg or Chekov are of this kind, and it is such works, whether novels or plays, that are most characteristic of intellectual Europe today.

We have already two such plays in Mr Lennox Robinson's *Round Table* and his *Crabbed Youth*; and it looks as if the audience that welcomed his *White-headed Boy* and the other plays in his old manner will give them a sufficient welcome. It is wavering; the shorter play it has delighted in, but the longer, which more openly calls in question a traditional point of view, leaves it a little cold. Mr Robinson has taught us to laugh at, and therefore to judge, a certain exaggeration of domesticity, a helpless clinging to the one resolute person that we had all perhaps noticed in some Irish house or other without knowing that we had noticed it.

He has not made his characters speak in dialect, for he is describing a characteristic that, though it may exist among peasants, needs a certain degree of leisure for its full display; one of those tragedies almost that only begin, as Maeterlinck said, when we have closed the door and lighted the lamp – almost a malady of contemplation. Should some other of our dramatists use the same form, he will have spent many years, like Mr Joyce or like Mr Lennox Robinson, in the educa-

tion of his judgment, and not only that he may keep his dialogue pure
without the protection of a particular form of speech, but that he may
judge where judgment has hitherto slept. Then he must be ready to
wait – his audience may be slow to understand – for a long time, it
may be, to do without all that pleasant companionship that belongs[34]
to those who are content only to laugh at those things that everybody
laughs at.

He will have to help him a company of players who, though they
are still masters of dialect alone, love work and experiment, and so
constantly surprise us by some unforeseen success, and a theatre that,
having no director or shareholder to pay, uses the profits on its more
popular plays to experiment with plays that may never make a profit
at all. The audience, though it has coarsened under the influence of
public events and constant political discussion, is yet proud of its in-
telligence and of its old hospitality, and may be won over in time. Yet
it may be a bitter struggle – one can never tell; as bitter as any Synge
had to endure. And you, perhaps, walking among your palm trees
under that Californian sunlight, may well ask yourself what it is that
compels a man to make his own cup bitter?[35]

Nationalism from the Abbey stage

THOMAS MacANNA

I don't mind making it clear from the start that I am, like Sean O'Casey's Seamus Shields, 'a bit of a Nationalist meself ... a Nationalist right enough,' and that to me the founding of a national theatre in Ireland was a necessary thing when it happened seventy years ago, and that same theatre a necessary part of the life of Ireland today. Indeed it has often seemed to me that, had Yeats and his companions not founded the Irish Literary Theatre and the societies that followed it, some other group of young, possibly more militant enthusiasts would have plunged ahead and done it. The spirit and urgings of the time demanded it. As it was, the separatists in the persons of MacDonagh and Martyn attempted to set up another, more avowedly nationalist theatre, but they were too late.

The New Abbey Theatre, built from Irish government funds and endowed with a reasonable and to some extent workable annual grant from the Department of Finance, is in fact owned and directed by a private limited company called the National Theatre Society Limited, which was founded in 1904 when Miss Horniman rescued both poets and players from what threatened to be a permanent amateur status by buying the old Mechanics Institute and renaming it the Abbey Theatre, for no other reason it would appear than the fact that its shabby Georgian façade was on Abbey Street. To this was added a grey, rather stately building on Marlborough Street, which had once been a savings bank, later a morgue, and which gave rise to the ballad lines :

It had many a life before it was a Theatre
It was once a Savings Bank and a Morgue sometime later
And the critics remarked with an air of great sufferance
That as far as they saw there was never any great difference
Will ye come, won't ye, will ye?
Won't ye come to the Abbey?

From a nationalistic point of view, the Mechanics Institute was singularly fitted to be a national theatre, though hardly a comfortable or elegant one. It had been for years called the 'People's Music Hall,' which has a good proletarian ring about it, but as a hall it had been let to many patriotic organisations including Young Ireland groups and later on the Fenians, and more interesting still, when the Dublin churches closed their doors on the mortal remains of the '98 leader, Terence Bellew McManus, when brought home from America in 1863, it was to the Mechanics Institute that the corpse of the dead patriot was brought after a magnificent funeral through the silent streets, and there laid in state under the green flag of the Republican Brotherhood. Much later still it was leased by T. B. Carrickford, an Irish touring actor (one of whose companies managed by, I think, a grandson, is still on the road in the remoter districts of Ireland), and with a strange sense of prophecy named 'The National Theatre.' It was the indefatigable Willie Fay who found the premises, acted as overseer to the renovations, and moved in with his players to open on 27 December 1904 with Yeats's *On Baile's Strand* and Lady Gregory's *Spreading the News*.

When the Irish Literary Theatre was founded in 1899 there were other theatres in Dublin at the time, the more respectable ones such as the Gaiety and the Royal presenting the best touring examples of what the London season had to offer, the less respectable ones showing music hall variety and melodrama. There was indeed no dearth of national sentiment on the melodramatic stages of the city. Rather the reverse: green-coated hero after hero was hunted and handcuffed, and in the more tragic pieces shot or hanged; chaste and beautiful heroines mourned for loved ones in jail, or in flight, or in Van Diemen's land; Michael Dwyer swung nightly from painted prison walls to effect his hairbreadth escape from the Sassenach; Robert Emmet faced his judges (sometimes twice nightly at 7 and 9), and innumerable Saggart Aroons and Mother Machrees suffered *cliché* after *cliché* in the interests of Kathleen Mavourneen, playing the harp and lamenting, again to quote O'Casey's Shields, 'Weep on, weep on, your hour is past.'

Dion Boucicault was more restrained but no less sentimental and his was the patriotism that assumed (in the best British fashion) that only those descended from noble Irish families (now, alas, fallen on evil times) were truly heroic, patriotic, or worthy of a happy ending with all fortunes restored, except of course freedom from alien domination.

And through all this shabby ritual, this endless and empty repetition of story and character and intention, there dances clumsily in his hob-nailed boots and his knee breeches and his swallow-tailed coat, the red-nosed, potato-faced figure of the stage Irishman. His beginnings are as obscure as the Anglo-American invention of the leprechaun; he seems the most necessary part of all this ridiculous dramatic industry, and even in his most refined appearances as, say, the Shaughraun or Myles na gCopaleen, he justly deserved the condemnation of Yeats and his friends. The Abbey Theatre put an end to him, although he died hard, and indeed can be found in a sort of stage-Irish summer in the technicolored musical films of Hollywood in the thirties and forties. Some near relatives of his turned up, real flesh and blood, in the literary life of Dublin in recent years, but that is a different story.

In any case, in 1899, one of the avowed aims of the Irish Literary Theatre was to 'show that Ireland is not the home of buffoonery and of easy sentiment, as it has been represented, but the home of an ancient idealism.'

Professor Saddlemyer has lectured on the background and events that led to the founding of the Abbey Theatre in 1904. My task is to examine the nationalistic plays that were presented on the Abbey stage. Before doing this, however, I should like to mention briefly the last performances of the Irish Literary Theatre at the Gaiety Theatre in October 1901 : Yeats's and Moore's three-act tragedy *Diarmad and Grania*, played by Frank Benson's professional English actors, and Douglas Hyde's *Casadh an tSugain* (*The Twisting of the Rope*) a curtain raiser played by a company of Dublin amateurs under Willie Fay's direction. But while *Diarmad and Grania* bogged down in heavy-handed professionalism, *Casadh an tSugain* soared with spirited youth and enthusiasm. It was fresh, it was lively, the Irish was simple and understandable, the audience understood it and loved it; equally important, the players understood it and loved it. The Irish amateurs were at home. It is important to note that the play was in Irish because this made it impossible to engage professionals for the production. But the reaction of the audience opened the eyes of the directors of the movement. More important still, Willie and Frank Fay, men of the theatre, inspired, as were the literary figures, by resurgent nationalism, made their first contact with Yeats and Lady Gregory. In the spring of 1902 the Fays disbanded their company, the Ormond Dramatic Society, and founded the Irish National Dramatic Society, the first time the word 'national' was used in connection with the stage in Ireland or England or the English-speaking world.

Professor Saddlemyer has spoken about the first productions of the society, AE's *Deirdre* and Yeats's *Cathleen ni Houlihan*. But although Willie Fay wrote later that the production of *Deirdre* 'gave to the Gael that which had never before existed in the history of the race – a means of expressing the national consciousness through the medium of the drama,' it has always seemed to me that the National Theatre of Ireland began on that April night almost seventy years ago when, in a far from elegant or theatrical temperance hall, an emotional rapport of electrifying intensity was created between play and audience at the entrance of Maud Gonne as Cathleen ni Houlihan. In behaviour she was far from the professional actress the Fays expected her to be: Frank anxiously peeped out through the curtain before the performance (when there was no sign of her backstage) and spied her parading through the audience in her costume, confident of her coming acclaim. 'Most unprofessional!' he muttered, but not to her. For she was truly Cathleen those nights, magnificent, beautiful, spellbinding. It was useless for the *Irish Independent* to insist that this was not acting in the accepted sense, that it was Maud Gonne 'the well-known political agitator': the audiece was with her and, after the unexpected laughter which greeted the peasant dialogue of the opening scenes, was frozen into an awed silence until the final lines.

Patriotic sentiment on the Dublin stage was automatically greeted with rounds of applause; here was something different. Here was silence and approval and a dimly shared feeling in the expectant darkness that the old woman was abroad in the land once again, that many were about to take hard service soon and count themselves well paid.

The hand of destiny or the fortuitous trends of the time brought Yeats to Lady Gregory, both to Willie Fay, all three to Miss Horniman, and finally in 1904 all four to the Abbey Theatre. The stage which had presented an emotional nationalism in *Cathleen ni Houlihan* continued, in the more respectable surroundings of the Mechanics, to show the same popular trend. Now, however, the dramatist is no longer Yeats, but Lady Gregory. Between 1904 and 1907 there are five plays, two of them masterpieces. *Kincora* comes first, an historical piece about Brian, the first of the empirical High Kings; then *The White Cockade, The Gaol Gate, The Rising of the Moon* (which soon gained the popular appeal of *Cathleen*), and finally *Dervorgilla*, a lovely play bathed in a mellow light of understanding and tragic realisation, but far removed from the stridency demanded by the nationalists. They even objected to the patriotism of the RIC sergeant in *The Rising of the Moon* as being illogical and unacceptable because of his uniform. But the nationalists attended the Abbey only at rare intervals. They didn't trust the Abbey; they were wary of its founders who were, after all, from the ascendancy classes, and they hated Synge.

John Millington Synge, Protestant, talented, and uninvolved, had already caused resentment and resignations with his *Shadow of the Glen* in 1903, and although his *Riders to the Sea* had been more or less accepted as an unimportant and certainly not very dramatic 'trifle,' there was unease when his name came up, a feeling (always at hand at the mention of James Joyce or O'Casey or Brendan Behan in our own generation) that 'he was lettin' down the Irish.' True indeed he did let us down, with a clatter and a bump, and left us ruefully contemplating ourselves in his darkly burnished mirror. Athur Griffith, leader of Sinn Fein and editor of *The United Irishman,* denounced Synge at every opportunity and lauded the lesser writers such as William Boyle and Padraic Colum. Even before *The Playboy.*

The story of *The Playboy* riots is well known; as well as Lady Gregory's telegram to Yeats in Glasgow: 'Audience broke up in disorder at the word shift. What shall I do?', and his reply 'Keep it on !,' whether the shift or the play has never been made clear. But although attendance dropped, the nationalists lost. What they wanted as an Irish theatre is clearly stated by many writers in *The United Irishman*; in a way an expectation of another kind of theatre well before its time, the polemical propagandist theatre of the Brechts and the Piscators of Europe in a much later generation, already foreshadowed a little by Bernard Shaw. Synge had shown the beautiful Cathleen bereft of green cloak and golden crown and, had the nationalists only seen it then, was bringing to the Abbey stage the unclouded vision of the artist who never takes sides, who stands in his own lonely circle and has no merchandise but truth, and who serves a nation with as equal dedication and sincerity as the most ardent patriot. And in all this there was no thought of the bloodshed to come; it was still in the innocence of pre-1914, even though the Irish Republican Brotherhood was in secret conclave and their thoughts had little of make-believe about them; their merchandise was grim reality; their truth was to be every bit as real as Synge's.

One extraordinary thing is that despite the seemingly current idea that to be a good nationalist one had to be anti-Abbey, Thomas Mac-Donagh, schoolmaster and poet, one of the Brotherhood, has a play on the Abbey stage in 1908, prophetically titled *When the Dawn is Come*, in which he foretells with strange insight the events of a coming revolution. In 1913 we have *The King*, a play in Irish for children by Patrick Pearse, side by side with *The Post Office* by Rabindrath Tagore. Although Pearse foretold exactly the manner of his desired death in *The Singer* (presented at the Abbey much later), in this other little play performed by the pupils of Scoil Eanna, his dedicatedly nationalistic school, there can be found his whole philosophy of sacrifice and innocence : 'One man can free a people as one Man redeemed the world.' There is about this writing no melodramatic exuberance, but instead a lucid and terrifying simple acceptance of sacrifice and blood.

The romantics were still there of course; audiences had come back to see, for instance, *An Imaginary Conversation* by Conal O Riordan, although there were patriotic doubts about the same writer's *The Piper*. Robert Emmet is the central figure of *An Imaginary Conversation* as he is of Lennox Robinson's *The Dreamers* in 1915. *John Bull's Other Island* is an offer in early 1916, but one can hardly count this as an expression of nationalism, the point being, as G. K. Chesterton pointed out at the time, that the Island was never at any time John Bull's.

We have somewhere in the archives of the Abbey a copy of the faded buff poster that advertised *The Mineral Workers* by William Boyle, *Spancel of Death* by J. M. Nally, and *Cathleen ni Houlihan* for Easter Monday 1916. The programme never went on. It was singularly appropriate that *Cathleen* was there and *Spancel of Death* (although never produced) was well named for the week. Barney Murphy, the stage prompter, went off to fight, as did Helena Moloney, a member of the company. Maire Nic Shiubhlaigh, although no longer a member, was with the women, and Arthur Shields, brother of Barry Fitzgerald, was in the GPO. *The Soldier's Song*, which was to be sung so often by the Irish garrisons during that bloody week and which eventually became the national anthem, was written by Peadar Kearney, a senior Abbey stage-hand.

The battle was joined, and in the middle of flames and devastation the grey theatre stood, strangely neutral, aloof and untouched. Neither side occupied it, buildings crashed around it, and when the heart of the city stood in ruins, gaunt and terrible, there it stood, snug and secure, locked and barred, still flaunting its extraordinarily relevant posters, not one pane of glass broken. St John Ervine, then manager of the theatre, came down to look at it in sheer astonishment, after the battle. 'I cursed the British Government,' he writes, 'and the crew of the gunboat *Helga* for their incompetence, and bitterly regretted that I had not come down on Easter Monday and fired the place myself!'

After the rebellion, when things were more or less normal again, Sir John Maxwell, who had ordered the executions, was brought backstage after a performance by some unthinking theatre official to meet the cast, but there was no one to meet. One by one the players slipped out of the green-room until he found himself addressing the silent walls. One player had been killed – Sean Connolly, the first Irish soldier to die. Shields and Helena Moloney were jailed, but Barney Murphy returned and continued to prompt as if nothing whatever had happened.

After 1916 things went on as before; seemingly normal play followed play. Lady Gregory seems to retreat into a fantasy land of dragons and giants and almost pantomime, an escape from bitterness and reality. She had lost her son Robert in the European war. In 1923, however, a little sadly and wistfully but with great lucidity and beauty, she pays her token to the dead, and to 1916, in *The Old Woman Remembers*, a simple ritual of lighting candles. From Yeats we have the poems and in 1919, although not produced at the Abbey until 1931, *The Dreaming of the Bones*. The play has an aloofness and a mystery at its core that can hold an audience, the small audience that Yeats always demanded, in awe and wonder. It is a play with an understanding of the distant and immediate past, yet one hesitates to label it national in the sense that *Cathleen* was and is national; in a way, Yeats in this play has transcended the very idea of nationalism.

In 1921 we have *The Revolutionist* by Terence MacSwiney, Lord Mayor of Cork, shortly to die on hunger strike in an English prison, and like Pearse and MacDonagh foreseeing his own death in an Abbey play. Another Corkman, Daniel Corkery, pays tribute to James Connolly in *The Labour Leader* in 1919. From all this turmoil of patriotic war and civil war great work would someday emerge, but, as Lennox Robinson mentions in his book *Curtain Up*, there were many scripts coming to the Abbey post-box with the good old-fashioned Boucicault themes of pure white Irish gunmen and coal-black British soldiery, and during the Civil War the inevitable themes of brother against brother and father against son. Denis Johnston in 1931 was to give the Abbey the best play about the Civil War, the ironic *Moon in the Yellow River* with its Chekhovian undertones and pre-echoes of Samuel Beckett. The same Johnston later gave the Abbey a fine 1916 play called *The Scythe and the Sunset*, but all that period belongs indisputably to Sean O'Casey.

O'Casey was a nationalist; he was also a socialist. His first published work was a paperbound history of the Citizen Army of which he was once secretary; his first play, *The Crimson in the Tri-colour*, full of noble socialists and despicable capitalists, was never produced. But his three great early plays stand supreme as chronicles of Dublin life and the Irish Wars. The first, *Shadow of a Gunman*, deals with the War of Independence; the second, *Juno and the Paycock*, with the Civil War, and *Plough and the Stars*, an example of early epic theatre, presents the glowing canvas of 1916. These plays follow a pattern: the first part of all three deals with people in slum tenements, their everyday agonies and frustrations. The war is something outside, on the streets, far away. In the second part of all three plays, however, the war comes on stage, grasps the innocent bystanders, changes their lives, involves them fully and utterly, and passes on. O'Casey takes no sides. He writes as he sees, his gifts are language and character; he deals with the people he knew during his Dublin days, the poor of the rotting slums. He stands aside, he does not get involved; like Synge he has his circle of truth. And like Synge he aroused the wrath of the nationalists who waited for the *Plough*, in the words of Yeats, to disgrace themselves again and rock the cradle of genius. The incident was innocent enough; like the earlier mention of 'shift,' it concerned the display of the Irish national flag in a pub. 'That flag NEVER saw the inside of a public house!' said a voice from the audience and the riot was on. This time it was the nationalist police who arrived to curb the turmoil, not the RIC. 'It's their own police this time,' said Yeats as the shouting grew.

One can list many plays in the twenties, thirties and forties that expressed both nationalistic theme and concern from the Abbey stage. The thirties reveal an impatience, a bitterness, and a sense of revolt against traditional lay and clerical authority, mostly in the fine plays of Paul Vincent Carroll, although his *White Steed* was rejected by Yeats because it exaggerated its effects to achieve its aim. *Remembered For Ever* by Bernard McGinn should be noted; it is a play of frustration at a lost idealism, somewhat reminiscent of the highly popular *This Other Eden* by Louis D'Alton in 1952, which adapted Shaw's theme of *John Bull* to a modern Ireland. The documentary play, historical and anti-romantic, made its appearance with *The Invincibles* by Frank O'Connor and Hugh Hunt in 1937, followed by two notable works by Roger McHugh, the prize-winning *Rossa* (1945) and *Trial at Green Street Courthouse* (1941). *The Great Pacificator* by Sigerson Clifford came in 1947 to give a tragic portrait of Daniel

O'Connell confronted by failure and famine, and earlier, in 1943, a most important play, *Lost Light* by Roibeard O Farachain, dealing in verse with the 1916 revolt, one of the few fully successful verse plays at the Abbey. Nor was the theatre quite finished with riots in the auditorium. During a performance of Seamus Byrne's *Design for a Head-stone* in 1950, the audience, although applauding the determination of the outlawed IRA to win complete freedom for Ireland, protested against the communist sentiments expressed by one of the characters in the play, aptly called Ructions. The play had a longer run than intended; whereas earlier audiences had stayed away following alleged outrage, the tendency now was to throng in to find out what it was all about.

There was another type of play in the post-Civil War period which, in artistic hands, brought a reluctant if almost Chekhovian mood to the Abbey stage when dealing with a time and a class fast fading into the twilight of Irish history, the old establishment class, the people of the Big House. Andrew Ganly treats them gently in his one-act *The Dear Queen* (1938), but Lennox Robinson is more analytic in his *Killycreggs in Twilight* (1937) and *The Big House* (1926). To conclude, one aspect of the theatre's policy, or lack of it, must be dwelt upon, especially when examining the last twenty years of its existence, and that is the Abbey Theatre and the Irish language.

It must be made clear at the start that the three founders of the movement wished to have plays performed in the Irish language. Twice in the 1898 declaration they say 'Celtic and Irish plays' and the adherence of Douglas Hyde to the Irish Literary Theatre made this wish of theirs a distinct possibility. At a banquet in 1900 given by the Irish National Literary Society to the Irish Literary Theatre, George Moore got to his feet and said: 'the performance of plays in our language is part and parcel of the idea which led up to the founding of the Irish Literary Theatre, and to emphasise this position, to make it clear to everyone, we are of the opinion that we should give a play in Irish. It will serve as a flag to lead to the restoration of our language as the literary and poetical language of this country.' In 1902 Frank Fay writes to Yeats in *The United Irishman* : 'for myself I cannot conceive it possible to achieve a National Theatre, except through the medium of the Irish language.' It was at first suggested that Douglas Hyde translate *The Land of Heart's Desire* into Irish, but fortunately he came forward with *Casadh an tSugain*, with what results we know. Two other plays by Hyde were performed and one, *Eilis agus an Bhean Deirce* (*Alice and the Beggarwoman*) by Peadar MacGinley. In 1912 Lady Gregory placed in the company a Gaelic-speaking actor who played in Hyde's *An Tincear agus an tSidheog* (*The Tinker and the Fairy*). But despite the intentions of the directors the truth of the matter is that no play in Irish was performed by the Abbey Company from 1912 to 1938.

In fact when a first-class play was written in Irish in 1927 by the young Michael Mac Liammour, the National Theatre of Ireland, the first to be endowed with a state grant in the English-speaking world, had neither the director nor the company nor indeed the inclination to put it on. In the event, *Diarmuid agus Grainne* was put on magnificently by Mac Liammour himself, when he founded, with state aid, the Irish-speaking theatre in Galway in 1928.

Since 1938, however, in fact since the advent of Ernest Blythe to the board of directors at the invitation of Yeats and the approval of the rest, the situation has changed. Ernest Blythe was the minister of finance in the first Free State government which endowed both the Abbey and the Taibhdhearc in Galway with an annual grant and so assured the continuance of the one and the founding of the other. His policy has been to build up over the years a company of first-class actors who can give performances in both Irish and English, and since 1938 well over fifty Irish plays, both one-act and three-act, some translated from European languages, but quite a few of them original plays well up to the standards of the English plays, have been presented. There was also from 1945 onwards a Christmas pantomime in Irish presented as an annual affair after the resounding success of the first experimental one, which was appropriately based on *The Golden Apple* by Lady Gregory.

Of course the theatre was attacked because of this policy; it was asserted that the standards of acting declined because now it was not a question of talent, but of knowing Irish. The Abbey has been attacked for being anti-national, anti-Irish, anti-Dublin Castle, anti-clerical, pro-government, and finally pro-Irish. It has sometimes seemed to be that the resentment against the theatre, assuming many guises over seventy years, stems from the very fact of its success and continuance – it is a very un-Irish trait to triumph over adversity, to win acclaim (even if it be mostly from abroad), and to continue to be what it is and what it should be in spite of everything. Had it died a heroic or even lingering death in say 1916 or after, its praise would be assured in ballad and song and story until the end of time. That its fame is assured while still alive and that it did not die is very un-Irish, and, understandably, resented by a nation that has always preferred dead heroes to living ones.

The Rising

ROGER McHUGH

My part in this conference is to speak primarily about the Irish rising of 1916 and to refer incidentally to its literary connections. These, of course, are many; they involve some of Yeats's poems, several of O'Casey's plays, and even some passages of Joyce. In *Finnegans Wake,* for example, one finds woven into the fourth or battle-theme paragraph the words 'phall if you but will, rise you must' and, shortly after this, a play upon the word 'phoenix'; since the phoenix was an emblem associated with the Fenian revolutionaries, it seems that Joyce was writing with more than phallic symbolism and was in fact referring to Ireland's repeated risings for freedom. An Irish poetess put it less obscurely in a poem in which Ireland speaks of her sons:

> She said, 'Ten times they fought for me,
> Ten times they strove with might and main,
> Ten times I saw them beaten down.
> Ten times they rose and fought again.'[1]

The rising of 1916 was the tenth of a series of struggles for independence that reached back beyond the English to the Normans and Danes. It was the fifth to unite the democratic with the national aim:

for the rising of 1798, under the influence of the American and French revolutions, had combined with the idea of separation the idea of equality, of social justice; the risings of Emmet, of 1848 (in which the most prominent writer was the socialist, James Fintan Lalor), of the Fenians (through men like O'Donovan Rossa), had continued this combination of ideas in varying measures. Its culmination in 1916 is best represented by the united leadership of Pearse and Connolly.

Originally, Pearse dwelt in his writings upon the separatist idea. As 1916 approached, he emphasised the importance of Lalor, 'the immediate ancestor of the specifically democratic part of that movement, embodied today in the more virile labour organisations,'[2] and it was probably under Connolly's influence that he wrote subsequently on the problem of property in one of his last pamphlets: 'no private right to property is good as against the public right of the nation. But the nation is under a moral obligation so to exercise its public right as to secure strictly equal rights and liberties to every man and woman within the nation.'[3]

Connolly, on the other hand, had long been a convinced socialist and moved in his writings of the same period towards a national position: 'The working class of Dublin stands for the cause of Ireland and the cause of Ireland is the cause of a separate and distinct nationality,' he wrote in *The Irish Worker* on 8 April 1916. Both of these men believed that the rule of empire, with consequent involvement in imperial wars, involved at least as much bloodshed as a rising against it.

In this they were echoed by Casement, who wrote epigrammatically 'Charity begins at home, imperialism in other men's homes; both may cover a multitude of sins.' We also find Pearse and Connolly in agreement that even if bloodshed preceded a military defeat, it might be necessary to awaken the conscience of the nation; this theme runs through Pearse's poems and plays and is stated explicitly in Connolly's editorials. Connolly's last remark to William O'Brien, as he left Liberty

Hall to occupy the General Post Office, was that they were going out to be butchered. 'Is there no chance of success?' asked O'Brien. 'None whatever,' said Connolly grimly.[4]

The rising of 1916, for any prospect of success, depended upon two things: the landing of a considerable quantity of arms from Germany and secondly a concerted rising of the Irish Volunteers which then numbered 12,000 men, combined with a rising of the few hundred men of Connolly's Irish Citizen Army. The first failed through the capture of the German arms ship, the *Aud*, and of Casement himself; the second because the commanding officer of the Irish Volunteers, on receipt of this news, cancelled the rising. But it took place because the extreme wing of the Irish Volunteers and of the Irish Republican Brotherhood had decided to go ahead in any case. In military terms this meant the confining of the rising to Dublin, instead of widespread guerrilla fighting throughout the country; and that some 1,500 men and 100 women opposed in Dublin some 2,500 British troops which were increased to about 5,000 within twenty-four hours. With 10,000 armed police (the Royal Irish Constabulary) to control the rest of the country it was a comparatively simple military operation to surround the few strong-points in Dublin occupied by the Republicans who, lacking numbers and artillery, managed to hold out for six days, during which half the centre of Dublin was reduced to ruins.

The surrender of the leaders was followed by their summary execution, which changed public opinion drastically.

> I write it out in a verse –
> MacDonagh and MacBride
> And Connolly and Pearse
> Now and in time to be,
> Wherever green is worn,
> Are changed, changed utterly.
> A terrible beauty is born.

This was no romantic statement. The first man shot in the rising was one of the actors of the Abbey Theatre and the change of opinion is exemplified by George Bernard Shaw's courageous publication in England of a letter about the executions: 'My own view ... is that the men who were shot in cold blood after their capture or surrender were prisoners of war, and that it was, therefore, entirely incorrect to slaughter them. ... An Irishman resorting to arms to achieve the independence of his country is doing only what Englishmen will do if it be their misfortune to be invaded and conquered by the Germans.'[5]

The change indicated by Yeats was perhaps best expressed in contemporary prose by Ernie O'Malley in his autobiography: 'Something strange stirred in the people, some feeling long since buried, a sense of communion with the fighting dead generations, for the dead walked around again. ... Without guidance or direction, moving as if to clarify itself, nebulous, forming, reforming, the strange rebirth took place. ... Now was the lyrical stage ... a strange love was born that for some was never to die till they lay stiff on the hillside or in quicklime near a barrack-wall. ... Always Ireland, Ireland, Ireland: story, legend, song, poem, planning. Perhaps we, too, would get a chance to fight or die. That seemed to be the end of all, the beckoning fate.'[6]

For two young Cork thinkers of the time there was suddenly a new perspective. Frank O'Connor has recorded his youthful feelings in his autobiography:

In April 1916 a handful of Irishmen took over the city of Dublin and were finally surrounded and overwhelmed by British troops with artillery. The daily papers showed Dublin as they showed Belgian cities destroyed by the Germans, as smoking ruins inhabited by men with rifles and machine guns. At first my only reaction was horror that Irishmen could commit such a crime against England. I was sure that phase had ended with the Boer War in which Father had fought, because one of his favourite songs said so:

You used to call us traitors because of agitators,
But you can't call us traitors now.

But the English were calling us traitors again, and they seemed to be right. It was a difficult situation for a boy of twelve with no spiritual homeland but that of the English public schools, and no real friends but those imaginary friends he knew there. I had defended their code of honour with nothing to support me but faith, and now, even if the miracle happened and Big Tim Fahy returned from Chicago with bags of money and sent me to school in England, I should be looked on with distrust – almost, God help me, as if I were a German who said '*Donner und Blitzen,*' which was what all Germans said.

The English shot the first batch of Irish leaders, and this was a worse shock, for the newspapers said – the pro-British ones with a sneer – that several of them had been poets, and I was in favour of poets. One of them, Patrick Pearse, on the night before his execution had written some poems, one of them to his mother – which showed him a man of nice feeling – and another, which contained lines I still remember :

The beauty of this world hath made me sad –
This beauty that will pass.
Sometimes my heart hath shaken with great joy
To see a leaping squirrel in a tree,
Or a red ladybird upon a stalk ...

What made it worse was that most of his poetry had been written in Irish, the language I had abandoned in favour of Flemish. And Corkery, who had introduced me to Irish, I had not seen for years. But I still had an old primer that had been thrown into a corner, and I started trying to re-learn all that I had forgotten. A revolution had begun in Ireland, but it was nothing to the revolution that had begun in me. It is only in the imagination that the great tragedies take place, and I had only my imagination to live in.[7]

Almost identical was the experience of Sean O'Faolain as recorded in his autobiography :

My heart did not burst with excitement and joy when I heard that a rising had broken out in Dublin that Easter Monday morning of 1916. I had not more than a week before seen somebody, who might have been Pádraig ÓDomhnaill, drilling a shamble of forty or fifty men in the open place beneath our windows in Half Moon Street – rudely accoutred fellows, with no uniform other than a belt around their ordinary working Pádraig ODomhnaill, drilling a shamble of forty or fifty men in the open clothes, only a very few bearing rifles. As I watched them fumble and stumble my blood had curled against them, they were so shabby, so absurd, so awkward, so unheroic-looking. They were, as my father said, as the Man would have said, disgracing our country : and this while real war was flashing and booming in Flanders and France. When we heard of the Rising my father and I raged at its betrayal. The British Army would clean 'those fellows' up in twenty-four hours. Then they would all get what they damn well deserved – the low ruffians, the common corner-boys ! Only bit by bit did my loyalties veer as the days passed, one by one, and I found that they were still holding out. Dublin was shelled and burning, that noble city I had traversed with poor Tom Boyhan, now dead in France, but still they were still holding out. There was a charge by British calvalry down O'Connell Street, in the best G. A. Henty, Light Brigade tradition of gallant lunacy, and I, who should have been all for that splendid gesture, felt the world turning around in my stomach when I heard, with satisfaction, that the ruffians and corner-boys had mowed them down. I continued to resist until the final surrender, and that broke me. Irishmen were surrendering to Englishmen, with dignity. That day I stole away up to my attic, and knelt on the scrubbed floor and looked out over the roofs of Cork under its tent of clouds, and I wept for them. When, in the following weeks, the British took out the leaders and shot them in ones, and twos, and threes, everybody and everything I had believed in began to tumble about me.[8]

Both these men were subsequently to become republican guerrillas and to write, probing, as sensitive writers do, into the deeper aspects of war.

Of course, the casual comedy of life went on despite the upheaval in Dublin. The average citizen saw little except fragments of the total situation. For me, as a small boy, it meant a spoiled walk on that Easter Monday when a red-faced man rushed up to my grandfather, who intended to take my brother and myself into town, and shouted, "The rebels is in the GPO!' It also meant a strange and sudden change in the nuns who taught us, a French order with many Irish sisters. Before this, the ultimate ambition which they set before us was to go up to Clongowes College and then, perhaps, into the English or the Indian civil service; after it they taught us many rebel ballads, which we but dimly understood until a few years later, when the Black and Tan terror in Dublin suddenly made it a matter of 'them' and 'us.'

A few years ago I gathered together in an anthology (*Dublin 1916*) a number of eyewitness accounts of the rising as experienced by a variety of people. There was, for example, Miss Stokes, English in sympathy, who found herself contemplating with equal horror a little boy of twelve, shot through the abdomen while giving water to a wounded British soldier, and two rebels lying dead, hand in hand, near the GPO under a green flag which somebody had thrown over them. 'The leader in Bolands [Mill] is a fine looking man called the Mexican,' she recorded with some surprise, 'he is educated and speaks like a gentleman.' This leader was Eamon de Valera. A visitor from England on the first day of the rising noted a large Irish policeman sauntering on his leisurely beat. When another policeman rushed up to him shouting that the rebels had seized the GPO, he quietly replied 'Begorrah, that's quare work,' and proceeded exactly as before. In Dublin Castle hospital a pro-British nurse saw James Connolly brought in wounded and wondered at his gentleness. Near the Gresham Hotel Sir Henry Lytton of the D'Oyly Carte Opera Company, who had created the part of Ko-ko in *The Mikado*, was allowed through a military barricade when one officer said 'Let him through, it's old Ko-ko.' In North King Street a number of British military ran amok and shot all the men in one row of houses, although ironically several of them had relatives fighting in the British army in Flanders. In another part of the city a youth of eighteen, armed only with a pike, was ordered to stop a tram which was needed for a barricade. He did so, despite severe misgivings about what he would do if the tram refused to stop. Later, after the surrender, as he marched down Mount Street behind his commandant, de Valera, he was grabbed by a large motherly woman 'determined to save the child from being shot' and had to kick her vigorously on the shins before he was allowed to rejoin his comrades. In Portobello barracks, a wellknown pacifist, Francis Sheehy Skeffington, was summarily shot by an officer who was subsequently found 'guilty but insane.' Soon Eva Gore-Booth was visiting Constance Markievicz in prison and so the two subjects of one of Yeats's poems were brought together in a very different setting:

> The light of evening, Lissadell,
> Great windows open to the south,
> Two girls in silk kimonos, both
> Beautiful, one a gazelle.
> But a raving autumn shears
> Blossom from the summer's wreath;
> The older is condemned to death,
> Pardoned, drags out lonely years
> Conspiring among the ignorant.

I am sometimes amused at the patronising tone adopted by scholars towards such women; there is an underlying assumption that because they didn't do exactly what Yeats thought they should have done they were wasting their time. In the dull academic lexicon of age, is there no such word as altruism? Maud Gonne is a case in point; her histrionic qualities are emphasised and it is seldom recognised that she could have an easy and comfortable life of it if she had thought only of herself and not of poor people thrown out of their houses at the will of their landlords. The attitude to which I refer seems to me to be born of a false identification which compels some scholars, where Synge or Yeats or O'Casey is involved, to climb into the ring in their defence when the need for such defence has passed.

But, of course, partisanship applies also to our own attitudes to the rising. In some ways it causes us to take it too seriously; I mean that the lighter and gayer side of it (except perhaps in the case of *The Plough and the Stars*) has not received much attention. I recall asking one republican fighter of those days what he thought of Yeats's query,

I lie awake night after night ...
Did that play of mine send out
Certain men the English shot?

'He should have slept,' said my friend. 'Dying for Caitlin Ni hUllachain did not appeal to us, nor indeed going out naked against the foe like the hero in one of Pearse's plays. Believe it or not, we wanted to *win*.' He also recalled his group of republican guerrillas sitting one frosty dawn around a police barracks. Inside sat the police, armed with rifles, hand-grenades, and revolvers, securely and comfortably frying bacon and eggs; outside were the republicans, a mere handful, armed only with shotguns. Presently their leader called out impressively, 'Surrender in the name of the Irish Republic!' No reply came from the police except the smell of breakfast. Again the leader called on the police to surrender, with the same result. When he tried it the third time one of his hungry and frozen companions lost patience, 'Will you for Christ's sake shut up, man,' he said, 'or you'll have the bloody lot out on top of us!' But perhaps the classic ironical story is that of Erskine Childers, formerly a British army officer, later fighting on the republican side and manning a barricade with a few supporters. As the British military advanced in formidable ranks, Childers suddenly realised that his companions had effected a strategic withdrawal and that he was alone. 'Come back, you Irish cowards!' he shouted in his English accent as he emptied his rifle at the advancing British troops.

In another way the rising has not been treated seriously enough by our own people. The Civil War, of course, was partly responsible for this. Our two big political parties grew out of this division and for many of my generation whose boyhood heroes were Michael Collins and Cathal Brugha, who died on different sides in the Civil War, the tendency was to cry 'A plague on both your houses!' Also, perhaps, as students we had read Frank O'Connor's *Guests of the Nation* and Sean O'Faolain's *Midsummer Night's Madness,* or the books of Liam O'Flaherty or Peadar O'Donnell, in which there is a probing towards the human values which are warped or short-circuited by war. We viewed with dislike the type of politician who played his 'national record' over loudspeakers at election time. The real veterans were respected, though as the years passed we felt a certain obsolescence and pathos about them. Donagh MacDonagh (son of the executed leader) has expressed this feeling in his poem *The Veterans* :

So these, who in the sixteenth year of the century
Saw their city, a Phoenix upturned,
Settled under her ashes and bury
Hearts and brains that more frantically burned
Than the town they destroyed, have with the corrosion of time.
Spent more than they earned;

And with their youth has shrunk their singular mystery
Which for one week set them in the pulse of the age,
Their spring adventure petrified in history,
A line on a page,
Betrayed into the hands of students who question
Oppressed and oppressor's rage.

There is a quotation from William Morris's *News from Nowhere* which I think sums up the dilemma of my generation: 'Men fought and lost the battle and the thing they fought for comes about in spite of their defeat; and when it comes turns out not what they meant and other men have to fight for the same thing after a different name.' Those of us who were interested in politics looked back and saw the two principles to which I have already referred as the vital principles of the rising: the idea of national independence for the whole of Ireland and the idea of some form of social system which would ensure the equality of treatment promised by the 1916 Proclamation.

We had got neither. The treaty led to the partition of Ireland and the two states of twenty-six and of six counties. The official declaration of the Irish Republic for twenty-six counties did not substantially alter matters and the border remains. The second we did not get either, although many of our essential services are in fact state-owned. The opening of equal opportunities to all citizens through education remained until recently a neglected part of government policy. But on both sides of the border things are moving today. In the Six Counties a strong civil rights movement, supported by people of all creeds and classes, is putting a colonial and sectarian government to the test. In the twenty-six counties there is now a determined movement towards a full socialist policy. On both sides of the border the ecumenical movement is sawing away the supports of conservative clerics. So eventually it seems that the aims of the rising may be achieved.

I have alluded briefly to some of its effects on our writing. Of course the Civil War brought a harder and more ironical note, a more intensive examination of our own consciences. The rising itself in one way meant not only the end of the 'lyrical phase' of Irish insurrection, but the end of the Irish literary revival because it began a period of upheaval in which a concerted literary movement could not flourish. Nevertheless, by that time the standards had been set, most of our great literary landmarks had appeared and the writer of today takes them for granted as part of his own literary background, while the more individual writers perhaps try to get from under their shadows and to create other standards of equal validity. If today reference to the rising is likely to barb the poet's shaft (Kinsella's 'Nightwalker,' John Montague's 'Patriotic Suite,' and many of Austin Clarke's poems provide some instances) this is inevitable; for its leaders, like Yeats's Seanchan, 'commended wasteful virtues,' which are worth recalling during its prosaic aftermath.

Sean O'Casey and the higher nationalism: the desecration of Ireland's household gods

DAVID KRAUSE

The rebirth of a nation's literature, to extend the irony of Denis Johnston, is not an immaculate conception. It is a painful process of renewal that grows out of attrition and contention, a civil war of violent words and conflicting aspirations. Therefore, instead of presuming to interpret the Irish literary renaissance as a predestined revelation of the Celtic mystique, whatever that might be, or daring to provide a capsule account of all the volatile forces involved in that complex process, I want to limit myself to what I believe to be the period of crisis – the catalytic stage during the first quarter of the twentieth century when the nation's new literature began to emerge out of the seemingly irreconcilable struggle between political necessity and the creative imagination.

Paradoxically, though Irish nationalism and literature had an urgent need of each other's vitality and vision, their spokesmen were from the start suspicious of their respective methods and values; they were sharply divided by the common goal of seeking to reassert the national heritage and pride. On the nationalist side, there was the hortatory attempt of the political apologist to glorify individual behaviour in terms of a purification and idealisation of national life; and on the literary side, there was the imaginative attempt of the artist to express his own vision of experience in terms of the reality of national life. Militant nationalism often seems at the point of winning the struggle, especially during a revolutionary period, when in the name of national honour the writers are urged to celebrate the proposition that all the men are courageous patriots, all the women are paragons of virtue, and love of country is the greatest glory. But even when they have been inspired by unimpeachable principles of revolutionary justice, such attempts to canonise the national character ironically threaten to become the occasion of national hypocrisy. They also become the inevitable target of those uncompromising writers who gain the final victory because they owe their Irish allegiance to what might be called the higher nationalism – the search for the truth about man, the quintessential nature of his character and his world.

In Ireland at the turn of the twentieth century, the development of the literary renaissance and the movement for national independence naturally coincided after the death of Parnell, each force guiding and inspiring the other in the early days as they worked towards the common goal of liberating the country from British domination. Nevertheless, it soon became clear that literature and nationalism were destined to collide with each other when they weren't colliding with Britain. The record of that internal collision can be observed in the lives and works of Ireland's major writers, Yeats and Synge, Joyce and O'Casey, four men who stubbornly maintained their loyalty to the higher nationalism. What W. R. Rodgers once wrote about Synge effectively expresses the writer's responsibility to his nation: 'A writer's first duty to his country is disloyalty, and Synge did his duty by Ireland in presenting her as he found her and not as she wished to be found.' Synge is the seminal figure, and this view has its roots in Yeats's comment on the genius of Synge and the way it exposes the gap that exists between the artist and the nation: 'When a country produces a man of genius he is never what it wants or believes it wants; he is always unlike its idea of itself.'

Synge had raised the whole issue with his very first play, *In the*

Shadow of the Glen (1903), a mock-heroic portrait of Irish peasant life which was completely at odds with the country's romantic idea of itself. And Yeats was also early in the field. On the controversial occasion of that first performance of Synge's play, presented by Yeats's Irish National Theatre Society at Molesworth Hall on 8 October 1903, the company also performed the première of Yeats's new play, *The King's Threshold*, which could be described as an ironic comment on, perhaps even a recantation of, his glowingly nationalistic play of the previous year, *Cathleen ni Houlihan*. It was no surprise, then, that Synge and Yeats were accused of disloyalty to Ireland by the Dublin newspapers, the self-appointed guardians of the national honour and were vehemently attacked by Arthur Griffith, one of the leading apostles of the new nationalism. Founder of Sinn Fein, the formidable Griffith, in the 17 October 1903 issue of his nationalist weekly, *The United Irishman*, launched the first of his unrelenting assaults against Synge and Yeats and the new theatre movement. About Synge's play he wrote the following comment:

The Irish National Theatre Society was ill-advised when it decided to give its imprimatur to such a play as 'In a Wicklow Glen' [*In the Shadow of the Glen*]. The play has an Irish name, but it is no more Irish than the Decameron. It is a staging of a corrupt version of that world-wide libel on womankind – the 'Widow of Ephesus,' which was made current in Ireland by the hedge-schoolmaster ... Mr Synge's play purports to attack 'our Irish institution, the loveless marriage' – a reprehensible institution but not one peculiar to Ireland. We believe the loveless marriage is something of an institution in France and Germany and even in the superior country across the way, and, if we recollect our books, it was something of an institution in that nursery of the arts – ancient Greece ... Man and woman in rural Ireland, according to Mr Synge, marry lacking love, and, as a consequence, the woman proves unfaithful. Mr Synge never found that in Irish life.

Well, hardly ever. Since Griffith subordinated literature to his quixotic defence of Irish womanhood, he was disinclined to judge Synge's play as a work of art. According to his national ideals, the play was a profane and dangerous foreign influence, a serious libel against Irish women, and therefore false. Nor was he alone in holding this chauvinistic view, for the performance of the play was greeted by some hissing and a minor disturbance when three prominent members of the Theatre Society who were in the audience walked out in protest and resigned from the company. Dr James H. Cousins, who was present at the time, accurately described the motive for the walk-out in the memoir he wrote with his wife, *We Two Together* (1950): 'Maud Gonne, Maire Quinn and Dudley Digges left the hall in protest against what they regarded as a decadent intrusion where the inspiration of idealism rather than the down pull of realism was needed.' The Irish artist, therefore, was a decadent intruder, and by these nationalistic standards a fabricated idealism was more palatable than the ironic reality.

If the three protesters had remained for the performance of Yeats's new play, they probably would have been exposed to another shock. They had all acted in his *Cathleen ni Houlihan* in 1902, with Maud Gonne in the title role of the heroic Old Woman who exhorts the men of 1798 to die a martyr's death for Ireland – 'They shall be remembered for ever.' But now in *The King's Threshold*, although he continued in the heroic mode, Yeats turned away from the national symbolism of Cathleen ni Houlihan and created a martyred poet as 'the inspiration of idealism,' the higher idealism of art. This Celtic parable is Yeats's manifesto in defence of poetry, an heroic defence of the poet's great gift of lyric power and his ancient right of high honour in the state. When King Guaire, following the advice of his national councillors, the bishops and soldiers and judges, insults the poet Seanchan by dismissing him from the state council – 'it is against their dignity/For a mere man of words to sit amongst them' – Seanchan acts to uphold his sacred right by going on a hunger strike on the palace steps. Rejecting all compromise as a defeat of his principles, he sacrifices his life for the belief that the arts must never be controlled or diminished by the state. At one point Seanchan reminds his disciples that poetry is 'One of the fragile, mighty things of God,/ That die at an insult'; and later he offers a Dionysian vision of the poet's great gift of tragic joy, a vision that owes more to Nietzsche than to nationalism :

> And I would have all know that when all falls
> In ruin, poetry calls out in joy,
> Being the scattering hand, the bursting pod,
> The victim's joy among the holy flame,
> God's laughter at the shattering of the world.

The later and major Yeats is prefigured in these apocalyptic lines. Only poetry can transform the tragic patterns of life and triumph over them, a mythical process of aesthetic joy which Yeats later embodied in such brilliant poems as 'Sailing to Byzantium' and 'Lapis Lazuli.' Seanchan's fight for the absolute supremacy of poetry led Una Ellis-Fermor to make the following comment on Yeats's aesthetic in her *Irish Dramatic Movement* (1939): 'It is a flaming exaltation of that vision which is the symbol of all spiritual knowledge and the gift of the spirit beside which all other values are disvalued. Poetry is either the root of life or it is nothing ... Even Brand himself never proclaimed more unflinchingly the doctrine of "all or nothing." ' In the light of such wisdom it is only surprising that Mrs Ellis-Fermor, instead of looking to Ibsen's Brand for a parallel to Yeats's Seanchan, did not more appropriately turn to Ibsen's great Irish disciple, James Joyce; for Seanchan is a blood-brother of Joyce and surely anticipates his martyred high priest of art, Stephen Dedalus. More precisely, perhaps the priority of kinship between Yeats and Joyce on the absolute supremacy of art should be reversed, with Joyce as the initiator of the principle. It was the young Joyce, disdainfully aloof from both the literary and national movements in Ireland at the turn of the century, who in 'The Day of the Rabblement' in 1901 had warned Yeats of the danger of allowing the Irish Theatre to become a part of the new nationalism. In that prophetic essay the nineteen-year-old Joyce had written with characteristic arrogance that 'Mr Yeats's treacherous instinct of adaptability must be blamed for his recent association with a platform from which even self-respect should have urged him to refrain.' By 1903 the disenchanted Yeats had created his 'all or nothing' Seanchan, and it would be fair to say that he had abandoned his not-so-treacherous 'instinct of adaptability' – with the national cause, and with men like Edward Martyn and George Moore who were grinding the wrong axes. Therefore, when Joyce in his 'all or nothing' essay went on to state the crux of the issue he was speaking to all Irish artists, he was invoking the fervour and dedication of a Seanchan and a Dedalus :

If an artist courts the favour of the multitude he cannot escape the contagion of its fetichism and deliberate self-deception, and if he joins in a popular movement he does so at his own risk. Therefore, the Irish Literary Theatre by its surrender to the trolls has cut itself adrift from the line of advancement. Until he has freed himself from the mean influences about him – sodden enthusiasm and clever insinuation and every flattering influence of vanity and low ambition – no man is an artist at all.

Needless to say, Yeats did not surrender to the Irish 'trolls,' those who distrusted and compromised the artist and were determined to limit literature to a subordinate position in the new Ireland. No less than Joyce, he spent the rest of his life fighting them, and Arthur Griffith was one of his first significant opponents. Predictably, then, Griffith did not like *The King's Threshold*, mainly because his sympathies were all with King Guaire and against what he called the 'selfish' poet who was foolishly and unreasonably fighting the wrong battle against the wrong enemy. Yeats wrote a formal reply, 'An Irish National Theatre and Three Sorts of Ignorance,' which Griffith printed in the 24 October 1903 issue of *The United Irishman*. In this article he defended his theatre and Synge from his version of trollism, the 'obscurantist' attacks of the three main pressure groups in Ireland that made it their mission to protect the national honour from the profane artist : the political, religious and Gaelic language propagandists. There is a direct parallel to this attitude in Joyce's *A Portrait of the Artist as a Young Man* (1916), when Stephen Dedalus, in rejecting the arguments of the nationalistic Davin, also identifies the triple-enemy of the artist : 'When the soul of a man is born in this country there are nets flung at it to hold it back from flight. You talk to me of nationality, language, religion. I shall try to fly by those nets.'

So Griffith had flung up his net. Thereafter he became even more narrowly nationalistic in his views, and he remained a thorn in the side of the Abbey Theatre. Several months after Yeats's article appeared, he wrote in a letter of 2 January 1904 to Lady Gregory : 'Did I tell you of my idea of challenging Griffith to debate with me in public our two policies – his that literature should be subordinate to nationalism, and mine that it must have its own ideal?'

That public debate did not materialise; nevertheless, the substance of the issue, literature *v.* nationalism, can be found not only in the heroic stance of Yeats's Seanchan and Joyce's Dedalus but also in the mock-heroic strutting of Synge's 'playboys' and O'Casey's 'paycocks.' For instead of defending the sanctity of the artist, these two playwrights instinctively adopted this idea as an implicit principle and went on to launch a comic attack upon the sanctity of the national idealism. As a result Synge and O'Casey were more violently controversial figures than Yeats and Joyce, though this was partly due to the fact that the theatre is a more public and more immediately provocative art form than poetry and fiction; and irreverent comedy is a more recognisably subversive weapon than literary martyrdom. This is in no way meant to belittle the massive influence of Yeats, or the versatile power of Joyce. Far from being limited to the arrogant aesthetics of Stephen Dedalus, for example, Joyce was a master of

comic irreverence in most of his works, particularly in his satiric ex-
posure of nationalistic follies in the hilarious Cyclops chapter of
Ulysses, where Bloom plays the sensitive mock-hero as comic scape-
goat at the expense of the roaring Citizen. But few Irishmen had the
opportunity to read Joyce during his lifetime when the unofficial
censorship kept his books hidden from most of the people, and Yeats's
verse plays never achieved popularity in the theatre and were actually
written to be performed in drawing-rooms for carefully chosen audiences of no more than fifty sympathetic listeners.

So we must turn to the plays of Synge, and even more to those
of O'Casey, performed in the Abbey Theatre to the accompaniment
of riots and protest demonstrations, to discover what amounted to a
comic desecration of Ireland's household gods. Under the banner
of the new nationalism those household gods or lesser deities – pieties
might be a more accurate term – were now equated with the sacredness of everything that was true-green Irish, from Cathleen ni Houlihan to Molly Malone. Though it was understandable and even
inevitable that the change should take place in a time of incipient
revolution, the impossible pieties of British domination had been
replaced in the popular mind by the improbable pieties of Irish idealism. Such a situation was ripe for comic desecration by courageous
writers like Synge and O'Casey who questioned and mocked the
inviolability of that idealism by relating it to the mundane and ironic
realities of Irish life. To the militant and moralistic guardans of the
household gods, such as Arthur Griffith and Maud Gonne, and their
counterparts out in force now across the land, these two playwrights
were guilty of a serious libel against Ireland; but in the hindsight of
history and the assessment of literary values it should be clear now
that Synge and O'Casey, though they are still regarded with suspicion
and enmity by some of their die-hard countrymen, were only guilty of
presenting Ireland 'as they found her and not as she wished to be
found.'

Synge found the Irish peasants in varying states of comic paralysis and contradictory tensions, straining under the complex moods of frustration and wild fantasy, vicarious exuberance and farcical despair, and therefore his dark comedies were a necessary desecration of those sentimental pieties of the idyllic and pure peasant life. One should have little difficulty in sympathising with the dispirited and potentially vibrant young Nora Burke, in *In the Shadow of the Glen*, over her inability to love her cold and cantankerous old husband, always wheezing like a sick old sheep and with nothing but rough words in his toothless mouth. She openly admits that she married him because he had a bit of a farm that might provide her only security against the fears of old age and insanity. She is terribly depressed and especially afraid of the threat of madness since even a mysterious and magnificent figure of a man like Patch Darcy was finally broken, driven to insanity and death in the desolate hills. And if she does not go the way of Patch, she will in all probability end up like Peggy Cavanagh, as she tells us in one of those dithyrambic sentences of Synge's which achieve a lyrical union of insight and tragicomic anguish : 'And saying to myself another time, to look on Peggy Cavanagh, who had the lightest hand at milking a cow that wouldn't be easy, or turning a cake, and there she is now walking round on the roads, or sitting in a dirty old house, with no teeth in her mouth, and no sense and no more hair than you'd see on a bit of a hill and they after burning the furze from it.'

With such prospects of tragic waste ahead of her, it is no surprise that Nora decides to go off with the poetic Tramp, who in spite of his fine 'blather' and his affinity with Patch Darcy can only give her an uncertain if immediate refuge from her sour and vindictive husband. Thus, the elaborate scheme of the mock-wake, the farcical revenge which Michael Burke concocts to trap Nora finally helps her to escape to her perilous freedom. By what parody of marital bliss and womanly virtue, then, did the nationalistic guardians of the household gods presume to lecture Synge that a woman like Nora should reflect 'the inspiration of idealism'?

But presume they did, and with such cumulative objections that *The Well of the Saints* (1905) was put down by Griffith as another anti-Irish attempt to imitate an alien and unsavoury story, this time from Petronius; *The Tinker's Wedding* (1907) was considered to be so outrageously 'beyond the beyonds' that it was never performed at the Abbey; and *The Playboy of the Western World* (1907) provoked a week of stormy riots in the theatre. Eleven days after the opening of *The Well of the Saints*, Yeats in a letter of 15 February 1905 to John Quinn wrote in part :

The audiences always seemed friendly, but the general atmosphere has for all that been one of intense hostility. Irish national literature, though it has produced many fine ballads and many novels written in the objective spirit of a ballad, has never produced an artistic personality in the modern sense of the word. Tom Moore was merely an incarnate social ambition. And Clarence Mangan differed merely from the impersonal ballad writers in being miserable ... We will have a hard fight before we can get the right of every man to see the world in his own way admitted. Synge is invaluable to us because he has that kind of intense narrow personality which necessarily raises the whole issue.

Synge and O'Casey, like Joyce and Yeats, carried on the fight for the artist's right to present his own vision of Ireland, for they were fiercely subjective men who provoked an atmosphere of intense hostility because they went against the grain of the national and patriotic sentiments. Refusing to pander to those sentiments, Synge and O'Casey created anti-heroic characters who had to fulfil their tragicomic aspirations beyond the conventional paths of Irish life. These playwrights desecrated the national character initially by the very fact that they chose to write sympathetically as well as ironically about cowards, hypocrites, liars, drunkards, tinkers, tramps, beggars, braggarts, parasites, and prostitutes, as well as an odd assortment of peasants, publicans, priests, pedlars, charwomen, carpenters, chicken butchers, bricklayers, poets, gunmen, hungry old men and women, and consumptive children. To such marginal people living for the most part on sheer guile and pride, the world of reality in early twentieth-century Ireland was something of a nightmare that could easily have driven them to madness or death. Their basic problems and needs were of necessity more personal than national, their impulses and desires were more earthy than ideal, and their only weapon for survival was an improvisational instinct for staying alive through comic resilience, a resourceful display of imagination and mendacious rhetoric which kept their tormentors off balance. It was only natural, then, that they could turn a deaf ear on pious principles with the same instinct for self-preservation that inspired Falstaff to cock an irreverent finger at an honourable corpse on the battlefield.

In *The Well of the Saints*, Synge's satiric parable on the vanity of human wishes, the religious miracle that temporarily restores the sight of the blind beggars, Martin and Mary Doul, reveals their follies and fantasies, as well as the cruelties of the villagers who mock and torment them with the merciless mirrors of reality; but it also convinces Martin that he is more likely to survive in the blind world of his unfettered imagination where his heightened senses allow him to 'feel' the joys and surprises of his vagrant adventures on the road – and that poetic choice is a greater miracle for him. Like Nora Burke, the Douls turn their backs on the sanctity of village life, they become itinerant exiles from the household pieties because experience has taught them a universal truth : a dangerous freedom is preferable to a safe incarceration. It was a similar decision which led Mary Byrne in *The Tinker's Wedding* to 'save' her son and his woman from the respectability and security of a proper Christian marriage so that they could all be free to follow the pagan pleasures of wild tinker life. And again it was a parallel choice which drove the miserable Christy Mahon to mock-parricide and mythic liberation in Synge's masterpiece, *The Playboy of the Western World*. After the repressed and adventure-starved villagers in Mayo transform Christy into a triumphant playboy because he 'murdered' his father in a daring act of defiance; after he is forced to 'kill' his father a second time in front of them and they suddenly turn against him, in the name of their outraged household gods; after he breaks free from their cruel torture and resurrects his playboy legend to become his own hero – after all this, it is his impetuous sweetheart, the tragic Pegeen Mike, who loses her nerve at the moment of crisis, Pegeen with her wild lamentations at the end of the play – 'Oh my grief, I've lost him surely, I've lost the only Playboy of the Western World.' – Pegeen who has been terribly defeated by her unfortunate loyalty to those enslaving household gods.

The victors in Synge's plays are forced to leave the community as tragicomic scapegoats who must improvise their hazardous freedom outside the norms of Irish society. They have liberated themselves, and the community, after it recovers from its ambivalent mood of outrage and loss, sinks back into its normal state of paralysis. Perhaps Synge's itinerant heroes are the original outsiders or rebels of the twentieth century, the early comic anarchists of modern literature. And behind them, behind O'Casey's tragicomic clowns, too, as an indirect and presiding influence, there is the archetypal desecrator of sacred things in Ireland, Oisin, the mock-heroic old warrior-poet of Celtic myth, the Playboy of the Pagan World as he appears in the medieval and later Oisin-Patrick dialogues, the *Agallamh Oisin agus Padraig* of dramatic ballad poetry. And in the line of descent from Oisin, there is also the mischievous and mock-heroic 'shaughraun' or vagabond of Dion Boucicault's Irish comedies, *The Colleen Bawn* (1860), *Arrah-na-Pogue* (1864), and *The Shaughraun* (1874), plays heavy with sentimentality but also so rich in comic invention, farcical irreverence, and sly Irish humour that they were admired and imitated by Synge and O'Casey.

When we come at last to the tragicomedies of O'Casey, plays dealing directly with the bloody events of the War of Independence, from the 1916 Rising to the Free State settlement in 1923, the desecration of Ireland's household gods increased in proportion to the accelerated fanaticism of Sinn Fein. From O'Casey's point of view, if the patriots were now the guardians of the national honour, the playwright had to be the guardian of the national honesty. No matter how noble the cause, death was a dirty business, and the attempt to die for one's country could bring out the worst as well as the best in men, particularly as it was seen through the eyes of the dispossessed poor people of the Dublin tenements. That was O'Casey's initial desecration, his decision to make the grotesque scapegoats of the slums his main concern instead of the patriots at the barricades, his refusal to sing the Sinn Fein slogans and wave the tri-colour flag. The disciples of Griffith and Maud Gonne never forgave him for these offences and he had to fight them throughout his long life, in his six-volume autobiography, a work full of mighty and profound desecrations, and in most of his later plays.

In his first play, *The Shadow of a Gunman* (1923), set in 1920 at the time of the guerrilla fighting between the IRA and the British forces, his chief spokesman is Seumas Shields, the anti-heroic pedlar and wise fool who can assess the ironic realities of Irish life and deflate the new pieties with painful accuracy. In his characteristic method of creating mock-heroes, O'Casey laughs at as well as with Shields, a man of exaggerated devotion who often uses his faith as a cloak for his cowardice, yet a man of insight and candour who is sickened by brutality and fears that the revolution is devouring its children. In discussing the war with his friend, Donal Davoren, the self-deceived sentimental poet pretending to be a gunman, Shields exposes the danger of fanatical patriotism :

I wish to God it was all over. The country is gone mad. Instead of counting their beads now they're countin' bullets; their Hail Marys and paternosters are burstin' bombs – burstin' bombs, an' the rattle of machine guns; petrol is their holy water; their Mass is a burnin' buildin'; their De Profundis is 'The Soldiers' Song'; an' their creed is, I believe in the gun almighty, maker of heaven an' earth – an' it's all for 'the glory o' God an' the honour o' Ireland.'

When Shields is reminded that he himself had once been a militant Republican – 'I remember the time when you yourself believed in nothing but the gun,' Davoren tells him – Shields justifies his past loyalty and present horror with the best of all possible replies:

Ay, when there wasn't a gun in the country; I've a different opinion now when there's nothin' but guns in the country – An' you daren't open your mouth, for Kathleen ni Houlihan is very different now to the woman who used to play the harp an' sing 'Weep on, weep on, your hour is past,' for she's a ragin' divil now, an' if you only look crooked at her you're sure of a punch in th' eye.

O'Casey was trespassing on sacred ground here by taking a crooked look at the new Cathleen ni Houlihan. The romantic and sentimental woman with the harp had been transformed into an angry and right-eous woman with a gun who demanded absolute loyalty and hit out savagely at anyone who doubted her ruthless methods. But the bold Shields, more effective with words than deeds, went on to question the heroism of her chief cohorts, the bloodthirsty gunmen, insisting that the defenceless people who were supposed to be saved by the war were becoming its main victims.

It's the civilians that suffer; when there's an ambush they don't know where to run. Shot in the back to save the British Empire, an' shot in the breast to save the soul of Ireland. I'm a Nationalist meself, right enough – a Nationalist right enough, but all the same – I'm a Nationalist right enough; I believe in the freedom of Ireland, an' that England has no right to be here, but I draw the line when I hear the gunmen blowin' about dyin' for the people, when it's the people that are dyin' for the gunmen! With all due respect to the gunmen, I don't want them to die for me.

The scepticism of Shields was O'Casey's humanistic attempt to measure the cost of patriotism. Although it is difficult to stem the tide of bloodshed in a time of war, he was outraged over the way the nationalist rhetoric ignored the indiscriminate slaughter. And in his next play, *Juno and the Paycock* (1925), dealing with the Civil War between the die-hard republicans and the free-staters in 1922, O'Casey moved on to another group of forgotten victims, the Irish mothers on both sides who lost their sons in the bitter fighting. In the stoical and proud figure of Juno Boyle he created his own symbol of Cathleen ni Houlihan, a black-shawled woman of the tenements who had a heart instead of a harp or a gun. When her son Johnny, who was crippled in the hip and lost an arm fighting in the Easter Rising, tells her he would gladly sacrifice himself again for Ireland, 'for a principle's a principle,' she also speaks for Ireland when she opposes his gesture of heroics with an ironic appeal to the higher reality: 'Ah, you lost your best principle, me boy, when you lost your arm; them's the only sort o' principles that's any good to a workin' man.' And later, when Johnny is slain by the republicans for the betrayal of his friend, Hughie Tancred, O'Casey again turns away from the stock responses of patriotic grief as Juno utters her classic lament for the higher idealism, the sacredness of life itself:

Maybe I didn't feel sorry enough for Mrs Tancred when her poor son was found as Johnny's been found now – because he was a Die-hard! Ah, why didn't I remember that then he wasn't a Die-hard or a Stater but only a poor dead son! It's well I remember all that she said – an' it's my turn to say it now: What was the pain I suffered, Johnny, bringin' you into the world to carry you to your cradle, to the pains I'll suffer carryin' you out o' the world to bring you to your grave! Mother o' God, Mother o' God, have pity on us all! Blessed Virgin, where were you when me darlin' son was riddled with bullets, when me darlin' son was riddled with bullets? Sacred Heart o' Jesus, take away our hearts o' stone, and give us hearts o' flesh ! Take away this murdherin' hate, an' give us Thine own eternal love !

With these elegaic words of anguish O'Casey had touched a universal nerve before which all appeals for national sacrifice must be held mute. For the Juno Boyles of Ireland and the world, suffering and slaughter are the immediate enemies of man. This theme was extended in O'Casey's next play, *The Plough and the Stars* (1926), in which he turned an ironic and irreverent eye upon the Easter Rising itself, one of the most significant moments of sacrifice in Irish history. Perhaps it was no surprise, then, that the mixed praise and hostility which had greeted his previous plays now exploded into riots in the theatre and provoked Yeats's famous 'You have disgraced yourselves again' speech to the protesting audience. The disgrace was nationalism's continuing attempt to intimidate and control literature in Ireland.

Again O'Casey had desecrated the household gods by identifying his Cathleen ni Houlihan with the ragged women of the Dublin tenements, with Nora Clitheroe and Ginnie Gogan and Bessie Burgess, instead of with the 1916 martyrs. This did not mean that he was against the revolution and the martyrs, it meant that he was for the forgotten mothers and wives. In the second act when the Figure at the street meeting outside the pub speaks the actual words of Patrick Pearse in exhorting the people to rebellion, three of the patriots in uniform come into the pub for a drink, Clitheroe and Brennan and Langon. They carry the national flags, and this, too, was interpreted by the rioters as a desecration of the national symbols, for we are to believe that the uniforms and flags never saw the inside of a pub; just as the appearance of the prostitute, Rosie Redmond, was a similar insult to Ireland, for we are to believe that no Irish girl ever laboured in that profession. The three men 'have been mesmerised by the fervency of the speeches,' they have heard the words of Pearse: 'Bloodshed is a cleansing and sanctifying thing, and the nation that regards it as the final horror has lost its manhood' – and over their drinks they cry out:

LIEUT. LANGON Th' time is rotten ripe for revolution.
CLITHEROE You have a mother, Langon.
LIEUT. LANGON Ireland is greater than a mother.
CAPT. BRENNAN You have a wife, Clitheroe.
CLITHEROE Ireland is greater than a wife.

But in the ironic context of the play, Ireland is no greater than her mothers and wives for whom bloodshed has indeed become the final horror. Juno Boyle made that point in her heartbreaking prayer to the Blessed Virgin, and Nora Clitheroe underscores it when she returns from an unsuccessful attempt to find her husband at the barricades and cries out wildly: 'An' there's no woman gives a son or a husband to be killed – if they say it, they're lyin', lyin' against God, Nature, an' against themselves!' The fierce honesty of Nora stands in contrast to the vanity and heroism of her husband, who sulked when he thought he had not been promoted to Commandant and later rushed out to die for Ireland in what his General called 'a gleam of glory.' Brennan brings the tragic news at the end of the play, and the irony grows darker with his empty words of hope: 'Mrs Clitheroe's grief will be a joy when she realises that she had a hero for a husband.' It is a meaningless heroism for poor Nora, who in her hysterical grief has lost her baby and her sanity, as well as her husband. Nor is there any joy for Ginnie Gogan, who lost her consumptive daughter, and Bessie Burgess, who lost her life trying to save Nora.

These tragic ironies reflect a major aspect of O'Casey's view of Ireland, yet they are balanced by a series of comic ironies which also desecrate the Cathleen ni Houlihan pieties and provide that comic view of life which allows some of the characters to survive and even achieve a degree of redemption amidst the disorder and death. This brings us to O'Casey's anti-heroes or clowns, men like Seumas Shields, Captain Boyle, Joxer Daly, Fluther Good, The Covey, and Peter Flynn – cowards and braggarts who manage to temper their folly with an instinctive shrewdness and wisdom that is attractive and reprehensible and human. Unlike Yeats's Seanchan and Joyce's Dedalus, they are unable to issue aesthetic manifestos and wage a private war against the Irish establishment; unlike Synge's peasants and tinkers, they cannot leave the community and seek their uncertain freedom on the road. They have been trapped in their Dublin tenements by a lifetime of poverty and hunger, and now by the terror of the revolution. They are only free in their own conception of themselves, in their eloquent lies and fantasies, in their selfish preservation of their lives in a ridiculous and dangerous world. What they do share with Synge's anti-heroes is their guile and bravado, their comic defences which function best in a spirit of anarchy and belligerent imagination. Their own type of guerilla warfare must be fought with words and mother-wit, the only weapons of the dispossessed; and, therefore, their lyrical and over-leaping rhetoric provides a vicarious gratification of their impossible dreams. The very language that Synge and O'Casey created for their characters must then be considered as an organic aspect of their tragicomic themes and structures.

Like Seumas Shields, all of O'Casey's clowns cross their eyes at Cathleen ni Houlihan; and in their irreverence they themselves become an essential part of the national symbolism they mock. They, too, are Ireland, with all their magnificent follies and outrageous derelictions of duty. O'Casey never lets them down lightly, constantly exposes them to satire as well as sympathy. Shields, whose conscience is seldom engaged and is only as honest as it suits him to be, unmasks himself as well as his countrymen when he declares : 'They've made Balor of the Evil Eye King of Ireland, an' so signs on it there's neither conscience nor honesty from one end of the country to the other.' Captain Boyle, that master of self-preserving hypocrisies and strutting masquerades, reveals his serious failures in the same breath that he asserts his anarchic freedom when, for example, he rebels against Juno's attempt to find out which pub he's hiding in to avoid the prospect of a job : 'Is a man not to be allowed to leave his house for a minute without havin' a pack o' spies, pimps an' informers cantherin' at his heels? ... I don't want the motions of me body to be watched the way an asthronomer ud watch a star.' Like his clever parasite, Joxer Daly, he is the cause as well as the victim of the 'chassis' that threatens to destroy him and his family. But for all their transgressions, these men also possess an indestructible spirit of fun and revelry which keeps them alive in a terrible time and reminds us that their frailties and fantasies could easily be ours under similar conditions.

It is central to the tragicomic genius of O'Casey that he is able to maintain his dual view of these grotesque clowns, mocking them for their irresponsible follies, admiring them for their irreverent victories. Therefore, the mock-heroics of the Captain are as much a part of Ireland as the stoical heroism of Juno. This was one of O'Casey's methods of resisting the nationalist pressures to idealise the Irish people. Perhaps he resisted those pressures most successfully in *The Plough and the Stars* by giving his derelict comedians a kind of left-handed heroism, which is richly shared by Ginnie Gogan and Bessie Burgess and Rosie Redmond, as well as by Peter Flynn and The Covey, and most of all by that wise and boozy lord of misrule, Fluther Good. Though they 'twart and torment' each other through most of the play, they are finally forced to unite and help each other when the street fighting and looting break out and they realise they have a common enemy in the war. They risk their lives for each other and some of them even die for each other; and thus they create their own ways of living and dying for Ireland.

Their mock-battles against each other also develop a further pattern of ironies, as in the second act pub scene, for one of many examples, when Pearse's call for the sacrifice of Irish blood is rewarded with a screaming hair-pulling brawl about illegitimacy and a quixotic fight over the honour of a prostitute. And this type of comic-ironic desecration must finally be linked to the mock-heroic deeds of that superb fool, Fluther Good, who could defend the honour of the prostitute and then go to bed with her; who could risk his life to save Nora and then take the same risk to loot a pub and become blind drunk; who could argue on all subjects with the grandiose illogic of a bragging buffoon and then silence the British soldiers with a devastating retort: 'Fight fair! A few hundhred scrawls o' chaps with a couple o' guns an' Rosary beads, again' a hundhred thousand thrained men with horse, fut, an' artillery – an' he wants us to fight fair! D'ye want us to come out in our skins an' throw stones?' There must be some redemption for such an Irishman.

Perhaps the rebirth of a nation cannot be celebrated apart from the rebirth of its literature; perhaps a nation needs the comic wisdom of its irreverent fools as well as the martyred blood of its patriots; perhaps Ireland was not ready for her freedom until her conception of herself was broad enough for the national character to encompass a Fluther Good as well as a Patrick Pearse. There are many ways to redeem Cathleen ni Houlihan besides dying for her, and Sean O'Casey dramatised some of them. In his own way he was the artist as total Irishman, and perhaps his was the higher nationalism.

Yeats, theatre, and nationalism

DAVID R. CLARK

'I am no Nationalist,' wrote Yeats in 1937, 'except in Ireland for passing reasons; State and Nation are the work of intellect, and when you
consider what comes before and after them they are, as Victor Hugo
said of something or other, not worth the blade of grass God gives for
the nest of the linnet.'[1]

Yeats was placing the nation, the creation of intellect, over against
the creations of God. Among the latter he included individual genius
and the consciousness of a people. Only in being true to his genius can
a man be true to his race. The man of genius 'must brood over his work
so long and so unbrokenly that he find there all his patriotism, all his
passion, his religion even ... until at last he can cry with Paracelsus,
"In this crust of bread I have found all the stars and all the heavens." '[2]
Unlike the nation, 'art, in its highest moments, is not a deliberate
creation, but the creation of intense feeling, of pure life; and every
feeling is the child of all past ages and would be different if even a
moment had been left out.'[3] Literary journalism and criticism, deliberate creations of the intellect, are only an unfortunate necessity
in moulding a national literature, for freeing the reader to understand the new and unexpected work. 'It is necessary to put so much
in order, to clear away so much, to explain so much, that somebody

may be moved by a thought or an image that is inexplicable as a wild creature.'[4]

Ireland must be freed of the prejudice that its national literature should be subject to cause or state. Yeats hoped that the beginning Irish dramatic movement might be 'a morning cockcrow to that impartial meditation about character and destiny we call the artistic life in a country where everybody, if we leave out the peasant who has his folk-songs and his music, has thought the arts useless unless they have helped some kind of political action, and has, therefore, lacked the pure joy that only comes out of things that have never been indentured to any cause.'[5]

'Though logic-choppers rule the town,
  And every man and maid and boy
  Has marked a distant object down,
  An aimless joy is a pure joy.'[6]

The national poet when he appears will follow the butterfly of his genius and not the gloomy bird of prey of his fellow citizens' preconceived ideas. He may be the opposite of his nation. 'There never have been men more unlike an Englishman's idea of himself than Keats and Shelley. ... We call certain minds creative because they are among the moulders of their nation and are not made upon its mould, and they resemble one another in this only – they have never been foreknown or fulfilled an expectation.'[7] 'National literature ... is the work of writers who are moulded by influences that are moulding their country, and who write out of so deep a life that they are accepted there in the end.'[8]

Being a creator, the artist is of necessity a destroyer. Like the god of nature, he shatters the old and builds the new. His creation of a national literature will inevitably challenge and offend the leaders of the crowd as they attempt to build the nation itself. 'Life, which in its essence is always surprising, always taking some new shape, always individualising, is nothing to [the newspaper, which] ... has to move men in squads, to keep them in uniform, with their faces to the right enemy, and enough hate in their hearts to make the muskets go off. It may know its business well, but its business is building and ours is shattering.'[9] Nevertheless, the artist builds more truly and permanently than these servants of abstract ideas because he is more sensitive to the inexplicable purposes of life.

It is this belief in being true to human life at its deepest level which lay behind Yeats's intent, in the theatre, 'to simplify both the form and colour of scenery and costume. ... An art is always at its greatest when it is most human.' 'We must simplify acting. ... We must from time to time substitute for the movements that the eye sees the nobler movements that the heart sees, the rhythmical movements that seem to flow up into the imagination from some deeper life than that of the individual soul.'[10] And his definition of a national theatre is quite uncompromisingly unnationalistic: 'that theatre where the capricious spirit that bloweth as it listeth has for a moment found a dwelling-place, has good right to call itself a National Theatre.'[11] These early utterances from 'The Irish Dramatic Movement' show the fresh enthusiasm and sweet optimism which marked Yeats's initial skirmishes in the 'embittered controversy which was to fill [his] life for years.'[12]

One is both amused and touched by Yeats's over-seriousness and over-confidence. He warns his opponents that the Everliving Spirits are on his side and not on theirs! In remonstrating with patriots who want what they call 'typical characters ... personifications of averages, of statistics, or even personified opinions. ... the ideal young peasant, or the true patriot, or the happy Irish wife, or the policeman of our prejudices,' Yeats cries out:

But is [Ireland] so very poor that she can afford no better literature than this? Perhaps so, but if it is a Spirit from beyond the world that decides when a nation shall awake into imaginative energy, and no philosopher has ever found what brings the moment, it cannot be for us to judge. It

may be coming upon us now, for it is certain that we have more writers
who are thinking, as men of letters understand thought, than we have
had for a century, and he who wilfully makes their work harder may be
setting himself against the purpose of that Spirit.'[13]

Yeats claimed little personal credit for the inspiration and establishment of the Irish Literary Theatre, modestly explaining that it was a
divine revelation. 'That strong imaginative energy comes among men
... because a genius greater than their own, and, it may be, without
their knowledge or their consent, has thrown its shadow upon them.'[14]
Apparently the founders of the theatre were in the situation of Leda
in relation to the swan. One likes to imagine George Moore, especially, in that role of Leda.

The concept of tragedy and of tragic character which Yeats developed and exemplified is consistent with these ideas. For Yeats literature was 'but praise of life,' not a criticism of life, and drama, both
'a farce and a tragedy are alike in this, that they are a moment of intense life ... an energy, an eddy of life purified from everything but
itself.'[15]

When the tide of life sinks low there are pictures ... life in the mirror
... but when Lucifer stands among his friends, when Villon sings his dead
ladies to so gallant a rhythm, when Timon makes his epitaph, we feel no
sorrow, for life herself has made one of her eternal gestures, has called
up into our hearts her energy that is eternal delight. In Ireland, where
the tide of life is rising, we turn, not to picture-making, but to the imagination of personality – to drama, gesture.[16]

For these reasons Lady Gregory rejected 'some play in the modern
manner sent to the Abbey Theatre' saying ' "Tragedy must be a joy
to the man who dies." '[17] The 'imagination of personality' is effected
in a literature which is 'the Forgiveness of Sin,' not 'the Accusation of
Sin.'[18] 'The character whose fortune we have been called in to see,

or the personality of the writer, must keep our sympathy, and whether it be farce or tragedy, we must laugh and weep with him and call down blessings on his head. ... It is no use telling us that the murderer and the betrayer do not deserve our sympathy. ... We are in the presence of a higher court. ... Before the curtain falls, a thousand ages, grown conscious in our sympathies, will have cried *Absolve te*.'[19] After all, 'there is no evil that men and women may not be driven into by their virtues ... '[20] 'Literature, which is a part of that charity that is the forgiveness of sins, will make us understand men no matter how little they conform to our expectations.'[21] 'When we find it becoming the Accusation of Sin ... literature has begun to change into something else.'[22] It is changing towards propaganda, towards leading articles, towards accursed opinions, towards the will doing the work of the imagination.

These ideas shaped Yeats's interpretation of Shakespeare. According to Yeats, Shakespeare knew that 'men are made useless to the State as often by abundance as by emptiness ... '[23] 'He saw ... in Richard II the defeat that awaits all, whether they be artist or saint, who find themselves where men ask of them a rough energy and have nothing to give but some contemplative virtue, whether lyrical fantasy, or sweetness of temper, or dreamy dignity, or love of God, or love of His creatures. He saw that such a man through sheer bewilderment and impatience can become as unjust or as violent as any common man, any Bolingbroke, or Prince John, and yet remain "that sweet lovely rose." '[24]

Yeats's analysis of Richard, though not without insight into Shakespeare, providing as it does a corrective and counter-emphasis to such criticism as Dowden's, is mainly valuable for what it tells us about the Yeatsean tragic hero. Some words about Richard from this analysis – 'a man's business may at times be revelation, and not reformation.'[25] – are put into the mouth of Martin Hearne in *The Unicorn from the Stars*, 'My business is not reformation but revelation.'[26] When Yeats asserts that 'Shakespeare's myth ... describes a wise man who was blind from very wisdom, and an empty man who thrust him from his place, and saw all that could be seen from very emptiness,'[27] we cannot help thinking of Yeats's Cuchulain, the imaginative man, misled by Conchubar, the rationalistic man, in *On Baile's Strand*, or Seanchan the poet and the narrowly practical King in *The King's Threshold*, or the hero Naoisi and King Conchubar in *Deirdre*. And when Yeats protests against those critics who are convinced 'that the common-place shall inherit the earth' and are filled with 'hatred of all that was abundant, extravagant, exuberant, of all that sets a sail for shipwreck ... ' one cannot help thinking of Forgael's doomed journey into *The Shadowy Waters* towards death and an immortal love.

Since the hero's catastrophe may have been caused by an abund-ance, a possession of 'certain qualities that are uncommon in all ages' rather than by a tragic flaw, a lack of 'some qualities that were doubt-less common among his scullions,'[28] it follows that his tragedy may indeed be a joy to him. The pose is familiar in the poems:

> A great man in his pride
> Confronting murderous men
> Casts derision upon
> Supersession of breath ... [29]

> ... Hamlet and Lear are gay;
> Gaiety transfiguring all that dread.[30]

Yeats's Cuchulain, he says of one performance of *On Baile's Strand*, seemed 'creative joy separated from fear.'[31]

In *The Green Helmet* he dramatised Cuchulain's heroism in the 'gusty energy' of that ballad measure which, he protests, had made Matthew Arnold complain of a translator of Homer that he 'had tried to write epic to the tune of "Yankee Doodle." '[32]

> And I choose the laughing lip
> That shall not turn from laughing, whatever rise or fall;
> The heart that grows no bitterer although betrayed by all;

The hand that loves to scatter; the life like a gambler's throw;
And these things I make prosper, till a day come that I know,
When heart and mind shall darken that the weak may end the strong,
And the long-remembering harpers have matter for their song.[33]

The essential thing which happens to the tragic hero as to the great
writer is that, like the saint, he moves beyond the individual will to a
higher apprehension. 'The heroes of Shakespeare,' he says, 'convey
to us ... the sudden enlargement of their vision, their ecstasy at the
approach of death ... '[34]

A poet creates tragedy from his own soul, that soul which is alike in all
men. It has not joy, as we understand that word, but ecstasy, which is
from the contemplation of things vaster than the individual and imperfectly seen, perhaps, by all those that still live. The masks of tragedy
contain neither character nor personal energy. ... Before the mind can
look out of their eyes the active will perishes. ... I think the motives of
tragedy are not related to action but to changes of state. ... Is not ecstasy
some fulfilment of the soul in itself, some slow or sudden expansion of it
like an overflowing well? Is not this what is meant by beauty?[35]

This achievement and this experience of hero, great poet, and saint
are what is missing in a writer of the second rank. In Shelley, for example, 'his system of thought was constructed by his logical faculty to
satisfy desire, not a symbolical revelation received after the suspension
of all desire. He could neither say with Dante, "His will is our peace,"
nor with Finn in the Irish story, "The best music is what happens." '[36]
In describing in 1922 how a writer like Dante or Villon achieves
greatness, Yeats comes very close to language which he had used in
1904 in heralding the Irish dramatic movement:

I know now that revelation is from the self, but from that age-long
memoried self, that shapes the elaborate shell of the mollusc and the

child in the womb, that teaches the birds to make their nest; and that genius is a crisis that joins that buried self for certain moments to our trivial daily mind. There are, indeed, personifying spirits that we had best call but Gates and Gate-keepers, because through their dramatic power they bring our souls to crisis, to Mask and Image. ... We have dreamed a foolish dream these many centuries in thinking that they value a life of contemplation, for they scorn that more than any possible life, unless it be but a name for the worst crisis of all. They have but one purpose, to bring their chosen man to the greatest obstacle he may confront without despair. They contrived Dante's banishment, and snatched away his Beatrice, and thrust Villon into the arms of harlots, and sent him to gather cronies at the foot of the gallows, that Dante and Villon might through passion become conjoint to their buried selves, turn all to Mask and Image, and so be phantoms in their own eyes. ... They and their sort alone earn contemplation, for it is only when the intellect has wrought the whole of life to drama, to crisis, that we may live for contemplation, and yet keep our intensity.[37]

The self from which revelation comes is associated with life. And 'genius is a crisis which joins that buried self for certain moments to our trivial daily mind.' It is only to the soul in isolation that genius may happen. It cannot happen to one whose thought is mere controversy. Style is won in secret, as is the moral strength of a great man of action. In writing of Thomas Davis, Yeats generalised that 'Books live almost entirely because of their style, and the men of action who inspire movements after they are dead are those whose hold upon impersonal emotion and law lifts them out of immediate circumstance.'[38] Yeats found his anti-self, his buried self, only when he had shut his door and lit his candle. Then he could invite 'a marmorean Muse, an art where no thought or emotion has come to mind because another man has thought or felt something different, for now there must be no reaction, action only, and the world must move my heart but to the heart's discovery of itself . . .'[39]

Thomas Davis's magnanimity, Yeats felt, was such an achievement. And it was paid for as the artist's must be by moments of tragic crisis in which he won self-conquest.[40] Davis, therefore, was, in this, on the side of life. However, most of the literature of Young Ireland, and most of its action for that matter, was mere controversy lacking the quality of life-giving genius. Yeats distinguishes between a love for Ireland which is 'the entire emotion for the place one grew up in' and the love for Ireland which is a mere idea, an abstraction. The former he finds in William Allingham, in Lady Gregory, and in John Synge. The latter he finds in Young Ireland and in George Moore. Synge's 'purity of genius' comes from his having been true to the instinctive love for Ireland and to that only. 'Emotion is always justified by time, thought hardly ever. It can only bring us back to emotion.' This is equivalent to saying that the mind should be true to what comes into it from its own deeper levels rather than to any idea or feeling caught from others. Yeats says of Synge and Lady Gregory, 'I have never known them to lose the self-possession of their intellects. The others ... possess their own thoughts above the general flood only for a season, and Moore has in addition an automatic combativeness that makes even his original thought a reaction not a creation.' It is this instinctive love of Ireland, love of life (which made Yeats as a child in Kensington long for earth from a road in Sligo that he might kiss it) which was lacking in Young Ireland, or rather which was replaced by an abstract idea. 'Davis ... was concerned with ideas of Ireland, with conscious patriotism. His Ireland was artificial, an idea built up in a couple of generations by a few commonplace men. This artificial idea has done me as much harm as the other has helped me.'[41] It was reaction, not creation, on the side of death rather than life, part of the trivial daily mind, estranged from 'that ancient Self.'[42]

These reasons led Yeats and his school to set James Clarence Mangan and Samuel Ferguson above Davis as poets, as Yeats explains in the important essay 'Poetry and Tradition' (1907).[43] However, it is clear from that essay that Yeats associates Davis with his ideal Ireland, rooted in tradition, and Davis's followers with the new Ireland, without tradition, which he abhors.

That love may be indignant, as in Christ's cleansing of the temple, and at the same time full of joy, is a difficult and sublime concept. Something like it is behind Yeats's appreciation of sweetness and magnanimity in his *Tribute to Thomas Davis*. Davises are rare. More usually because of a lack of love, 'a form of the eternal contemplation of what is,'[44]

abstract thoughts are raised up between men's minds and Nature ... till minds, whose patriotism is perhaps great enough to carry them to the scaffold, cry down natural impulse with the morbid persistence of minds unsettled by some fixed idea. They are preoccupied with the nation's future, with heroes, poets, soldiers, painters, armies, fleets, but only as these things are understood by a child in a National School, while a secret feeling that what is so unreal needs continual defence makes them bitter and restless. They are like some State which has only paper money, and seeks by punishments to make it buy whatever gold can buy. They no longer love, for only life is loved, and at last a generation is like an hysterical woman who will make unmeasured accusations and believe impossible things, because of some logical deduction from a solitary thought which has turned a portion of her mind to stone.[45]

We meet the hysterical woman again as Countess Markievicz in 'On a Political Prisoner' (1920) and as Maud Gonne bartering 'every good/ By quiet natures understood/For an old bellows full of angry wind' in 'A Prayer for My Daughter' (1919). 'Hysterical women' shrilly protest 'poets that are always gay' in 'Lapis Lazuli' (1938). The stone to which such a mind is turned is 'in the midst of all' in 'Easter 1916' and there troubles 'the living stream.'[46] Love, joy, and indignation are on the side of what lives and flourishes. Pity and hatred[47] are on the side of stony death.

Did Yeats's own writing life follow the pattern which he has des-

cribed in those of Dante and Villon? One thinks, of course, of his un-
requited love for Maud Gonne as the 'tragedy' of his personal life.
But there was another, perhaps greater, renunciation which he had to
make and that was his hope of creating in Ireland, through his Irish
dramatic movement, a unity of culture. In his attempt to realise unity
of culture in the nation of Ireland, he became a man of action.

One may see the years between *The Wind Among the Reeds* (1899)
when Yeats was thirty-four and *Responsibilities* (1914) when Yeats
was forty-nine, years which pretty much are the years of Yeats's preoccupation with the Irish dramatic movement, in one of two ways.
One may say that these are the years in which Yeats came to terms
with the world. Or one may say that these are the years in which Yeats
discovered his true character by growing disillusionment with the
role which he was playing. There is ground for feeling that Yeats considered his 'man of action' period to have been one in which he served
strange gods, a period of illusion, from which he retired knowing that
its chief value was that it taught him that his true role was not management of men but the lonely perfecting of an artifact. The man of
action was not to be triumphant in the world, but triumphant as
transformed into the persona of much of Yeats's middle and late
poetry.

Yeats's objectification of his dream as he took his place in the world
was successful only in revealing to him the insubstantiality of that
world. The later Yeats, withered into the truth, let the world wither
into it as well. The truth was not external multiplicity, but inner unity.
He took his place in the world, but then really turned away from the
world. Or rather he absorbed the world, allowed it to enter his meditation, but not to overwhelm or upset that meditation.

According to one of Yeats's last formulations in his 1937 'A General
Introduction for My Work,' the 'poet writes always of his personal
life,'[48] but he turns his private pathos or tragedy into a phantasmagoria of fictional events and personae which distances and impersonal-
ises it. In the style or attitude of his poetry he attempts to be as 'cold

and passionate as the dawn.'[49] He attempts this discipline in order to find and evoke beneath the personal and accidental self a more profound and universal identity, 'that ancient Self,' that he may speak to all men on the deepest level and of the most important and permanent subjects.

Moving from an individual to a national or historical perspective, he will find, if he is of the holy land of Ireland, that 'that ancient self' has wrought behind and in history 'a great tapestry,'[50] expressing through myth, folklore, and events the reality of the supernatural. Thus he can feel that he writes not only out of the deepest personal inspiration, but also 'out of a people to a people.'[51] There is nothing easy about this discipline. It is of all things not impossible the most difficult, and the concept explains that perpetual struggle between man and demon, between self and anti-self which informs so much of his verse and prose, and which as truly is the preoccupation of his drama.

A middle and a late play which deal with the national theme are *The Dreaming of the Bones* (1919) and *The Death of Cuchulain* (1939). The simpler case in this regard is *The Death of Cuchulain*, in which the Irish hero chooses to fight against impossible odds, suffers six mortal wounds, binds himself to a stone pillar that he may die standing, is approached by Aoife, the fierce warrior woman who is mother of his slain son and who wishes to kill him in vengeance, and is finally slain by the blind old beggar man of *On Baile's Strand* just as Cuchulain has the revelation that after death his soul will take the shape of a singing bird. Of the various critics whom I have read on *The Death of Cuchulain* the one who comes closest to my feeling about the play is Leonard Nathan in his *The Tragic Drama of W. B. Yeats*. He says:

Achilles' most tragic moment in *The Iliad* is not on the battlefield, but in his own quarters when, violating all 'popular' notions of the hero, he gives Priam back the greatest spoil of the war, his dead son, Hector. This generous gesture is accompanied by a deeply moving, rather quiet speech which shows Achilles' compassionate grasp of the human condition. Not even Priam truly understands what has happened, but for the first time in the epic someone has been courageous enough to feel and act on the profound and unpopular idea that, in E. M. W. Tillyard's words, 'in the utmost extremities the things that unite men are stronger than those that divide them.' Like Achilles, Cuchulain, in the face of his fate, exhibiting heroic generosity and heroic calm, is misunderstood. And he assumes that tone of reverie, which Yeats believed marked the tragic ecstasy, to say 'I say it is about to sing'; this prophecy suggests transfiguration for the hero, if only in the words of the poet who sings of his heroism.[52]

Cuchulain indeed, as his mistress Eithne Inguba says, lacks the passion necessary to human life. But this is not the same as 'weariness and indifference,' charges lodged against the play by Helen Vendler in her idea-packed book *Yeats's Vision and the Later Plays*.[53] I believe that Cuchulain has moved from the joy of passionate life to the ecstasy of contemplation. He can forgive, though not understand, Eithne Inguba; he can agree with Aoife's right to kill him while cherishing the memory of her beautiful veils and urging her not to spoil her veil by binding him with it; he can even accept his murderer for what he is without expressing either hatred or pity – 'I think you are a blind old man.'[54]

A passage which I quoted from Yeats less fully above is relevant:

Ecstasy ... is from the contemplation of things vaster than the individual and imperfectly seen, perhaps, by all those that still live. The masks of tragedy contain neither character nor personal energy. They are allied to decoration and to the abstract figures of Egyptian temples. Before the mind can look out of their eyes the active will perishes, hence their sorrowful calm. Joy is of the will which labours, which overcomes obstacles, which knows triumph. The soul knows its changes of state alone, and I think the motives of tragedy are not related to action but to changes of state.[55]

Cuchulain awaits his change to the 'soft feathery shape' of a bird, his 'soul's first shape,'[56] in a mood – and with imagery – reminiscent of *The Shadowy Waters* of many years before where 'Forgael and the woman,' according to Yeats's 1906 description in *The Arrow*, 'drifted on alone, following the birds, awaiting death and what comes after, or some mysterious transformation of the flesh, an embodiment of every lover's dream,'[57] or in a mood – and with imagery – reminiscent of his 1900 essay on 'The Philosophy of Shelley's Poetry':

This beauty, this divine order, whereof all things shall become a part in a kind of resurrection of the body, is already visible to the dead and to souls in ecstasy, for ecstasy is a kind of death. The dying Lionel [in Shelley's 'Rosalind and Helen'] hears the song of the nightingale, and cries:

Heardst thou not sweet words among
That heaven-resounding minstrelsy?
Heardst thou not, that those who die
Awake in a world of ecstasy?
That love, when limbs are interwoven,
And sleep, when the night of life is cloven,
And thought, to the world's dim boundaries clinging,
And music, when one beloved is singing,
Is death? Let us drain right joyously
The cup which the sweet bird fills for me.[58]

There are some parallels in the play between Cuchulain and the heroes of the Rising, more than merely the fact of the statue by Oliver Sheppard standing in the post office. There is the parallel for example of the last-minute uncertainty as to the plans for the battle, whether it was or was not to take place. Eithne Inguba's appearance with conflicting messages and Cuchulain's deliberate choice to fight with his small band against impossible odds are like the council of leaders' decision to go ahead with the Rising. The choice to fight against impossible odds is exemplified, moreover, in the case of the O'Rahilly, whom Yeats celebrates in his poem :

> Sing of the O'Rahilly
> That had such little sense
> He told Pearse and Connolly
> He'd gone to great expense
> Keeping all the Kerry men
> Out of that crazy fight;
> That he might be there himself
> Had travelled half the night.
> 　*How goes the weather?*
>
> 'Am I such a craven that
> I should not get the word
> But for what some travelling man
> Had heard I had not heard?'
> Then on Pearse and Connolly
> He fixed a bitter look :
> 'Because I helped to wind the clock
> I come to hear it strike.'
> 　*How goes the weather?*[59]

Cuchulain's magnanimity towards Eithne Inguba, Aoife, and the Blind Man are like Pearse's hope that the British would 'accept [his] single life in forfeiture and ... give a general amnesty to the brave men and boys who ... fought at [his] bidding' or like Connolly's prayer of forgiveness for the men who shot him.[60] And the mood of abstraction, almost exaltation, with which Cuchulain goes through his final scenes reminds me of the uncanny atmosphere of the hero's already having ascended to another life, an atmosphere of purest dedication to an ideal, an almost sleep-walking serenity, which one finds in such works as Pearse's 'The Singer.' Pearse, as described by a compatriot, had personally the same quality. Whereas Connolly 'was a restless, energetic figures ... Pearse, on the other hand, appeared to be "lost somewhere in the clouds"; at times "even looked supremely futile" ... Yet ... by his very presence alone, he added an untold value. There was an ambience about him which spread calm confidence. ... Wherever he went, the eyes of the garrison followed ... '[61] Both Pearse himself and the hero of his play – no doubt in part a self-portrait – may be viewed as going through their actions in a mood of tragic ecstasy.

Cuchulain and the heroes of the post office meet in that final light of tragedy where a terrible beauty is born. But they do not start from the same place. The Young Man who climbs to a desolate mountain spot in *The Dreaming of the Bones* has a far different motive from the Young Man (Cuchulain) who climbs to a like spot in *At the Hawk's Well*. The Young Man of *The Dreaming of the Bones* has not the 'lofty dissolute air' of Cuchulain, who has heard a 'story told over the wine towards dawn' and has immediately 'spread sail'[62] and has followed this whim 'most difficult/Among whims not possible'[63] in search of personal immortality. The Young Man of *The Dreaming of the Bones* has fought at the post office. Searching on the Galway coast for a hiding place, he stumbles on a spot haunted by the ghosts of Diarmuid and Dervorgilla, lovers who brought the Normans into Ireland 700 years ago in order to help Diarmuid in his fight with Dervorgilla's husband. The Young Man is one who, like Pearse, has self-forgettingly renounced the 'beauty of beauty'[64] and has set his face to the road before him, and if need be to the death that he shall meet. He has set his face to 'whatever task's most difficult/Among tasks not impossible.'[65] If he seeks immortality, it is not as fulfilment of personality, but its renunciation. He has taken the 'hard service' of Cathleen ni Houlihan and only through it shall he be 'remembered for ever ... [and] alive for ever.'[66] Although the complexity of his character is not developed, he no doubt exemplifies, as do Countess Markievicz in 'On a Political Prisoner' and Maud Gonne transformed into *The Countess Cathleen*, ' "the soul of one that loves Ireland ...

plunging into unrest, seeming to lose itself, to bargain itself away to the very wickedness of the world, and to surrender what is eternal for what is temporary." '67 These are all self-forgetful people. While composing *The Dreaming of the Bones* Yeats writes of Maud Gonne's being 'in a joyous and self forgetting condition of political hate the like of which I have not yet encountered.'68

Actually the Young Man differs from these heroines in that he starts as an objective mind dedicated to an abstract ideal and undergoes a temptation to become subjective and imaginative – to imagine so vividly the plight of Diarmuid and Dervorgilla that he forgives them and accepts what history has done to Ireland. The temptation of the 'Political Prisoner' and of the Countess Cathleen is just the opposite. It is Maud Gonne's temptation, as we have noted in connection with 'A Prayer for My Daughter,' to give up 'every good/By quiet natures understood/For an old bellows full of angry wind.'69 It is to cease to be imaginative daughters of the swan or rock-bred seaborne birds and become part of that logical objective horde of 'brazen hawks' whose 'innumerable clanging wings' have 'put out the moon.'70

In a sense their temptation is like that of Cuchulain in *At the Hawk's Well* when his quest for immortality becomes detoured into a crazy chase after the hawk woman and a crazy battle with the woman warriors she inspires. But in *At the Hawk's Well* the meanings relate to the life of the artist, rather than of the nationalist, to the perpetual inner battle Yeats had to fight against ruling ideas and to keep abstraction out of his poetry.

The temptation of the Young Man in *The Dreaming of the Bones* is that he will be magnanimous like the hero of *The Death of Cuchulain*, that he will achieve the imaginative height at which the artist's vision forgives all sins. He starts out as an objective mind which deals effectively with exterior things, whose notion of his duty is intense and simple. He is not concerned with the purgatorial life of the dead, but with the objective details relevant to his escape and with an oversimple abstract rationalism. Of the dead he says :

Well, let them dream into what shape they please
And fill waste mountains with the invisible tumult
Of the fantastic conscience. I have no dread;
They cannot put me into gaol or shoot me;
And seeing that their blood has returned to fields
That have grown red from drinking blood like mine,
They would not if they could betray.[71]

The unconscious irony of this speech is probably not lost upon Diarmuid and Dervorgilla, to whom he is speaking. The Young Man's danger is not, as he fears, from the guns of the living but from the dreaming of the bones. His danger is that his head will be lost in a cloud, that he will 'let the whole world go' as did Diarmuid and Dervorgilla, that hearing the 'wandering airy music' of their story, 'moidered in that snare,' he will be 'lost of a sudden,/In that sweet wandering snare,'[72] that like Dante in the Paolo and Francesca incident of the *Inferno* he will fall victim to the passionate mood of the lovers and be overcome; that he will forget the lovers' handiwork, what they have done to Ireland, as they have forgotten it.

The temptation of the Young Man is to see, in imagination, as in a play, the torment of the lovers who have betrayed Ireland, and to see it so vividly that the seeing amounts to understanding, forgiveness.

YOUNG MAN ... Why do you dance?
    Why do you gaze, and with so passionate eyes,
    One on the other; and then turn away,
    Covering your eyes, and weave it in a dance?
    Who are you? what are you? you are not natural.
YOUNG GIRL Seven hundred years our lips have never met.
YOUNG MAN Why do you look so strangely at one another,
    So strangely and so sweetly?
YOUNG GIRL Seven hundred years.
YOUNG MAN So strangely and so sweetly. All the ruin,

All, all their handiwork is blown away
As though the mountain air had blown it away
Because their eyes have met. They cannot hear,
Being folded up and hidden in their dance.
The dance is changing now. They have dropped their eyes,
They have covered up their eyes as though their hearts
Had suddenly been broken — never, never
Shall Diarmuid and Dervorgilla be forgiven.
They have drifted in the dance from rock to rock.
They have raised their hands as though to snatch the sleep
That lingers always in the abyss of the sky
Though they can never reach it. A cloud floats up
And covers all the mountain-head in a moment;
And now it lifts and they are swept away.

The Stranger and the Young Girl go out

I had almost yielded and forgiven it all —
Terrible the temptation and the place![73]

But he does not yield, nor forgive. It is not for him to free these sinners from the now visible tumult of their fantastic consciences. The concept is terribly Dantesque. The Young Man has now thoroughly visualised the lovers' situation and indeed sympathised with it. But the world, the landscape of ruined Ireland, their handiwork, has not vanished for him, as it has for them. As the complexity and power of the Paolo and Francesca story stem from the simultaneous presence of the passionate episode and the framework of justice in the background — so that when Francesca speaks of 'he, who shall never be divided from me' we are moved by the emotion and yet perceive that this togetherness is hell, just punishment[74] — just so the dance in which Diarmuid and Dervorgilla act their love and torment takes place before the backdrop of the Irish land, Irish history, a framework which places and diminishes the lovers' torment, reveals it as only a part of the whole picture.

So here we're on the summit. I can see
The Aran Islands, Connemara Hills,
And Galway in the breaking light; there too
The enemy has toppled roof and gable,
And torn the panelling from ancient rooms;
What generations of old men had known
Like their own hands, and children wondered at,
Has boiled a trooper's porridge. That town had lain,
But for the pair that you would have me pardon,
Amid its gables and its battlements
Like any old admired Italian town;
For though we have neither coal, nor iron ore,
To make us wealthy and corrupt the air,
Our country, if that crime were uncommitted,
Had been most beautiful.[75]

Yeats means us to feel, I think, that the Young Man has changed at the end of the play. He can no longer condemn easily the Irish who have betrayed Ireland. Diarmuid and Dervorgilla, even as traitors, are spirits of the land. Their dreams darken the sun of the living. Their stylised dance projects what Yeats in a passage quoted above called 'the nobler movements that the heart sees, the rhythmical movements that seem to flow up into the imagination from some deeper life than that of the individual soul.'[76] Their very 700 years of torment certifies these traitors as true Irishmen, since the conscience itself causes the soul's punishment. The Young Man had not known before the full depth and complexity of the great hatred and the great love in the little room of Ireland. He cannot condemn easily, simply, crudely any more. But he does condemn. Or rather he refuses to lift the condemnation which the lovers have given themselves.

I think that Yeats hopes that his hero has been freed from opinionated, leading-article thinking, and at the same time has retained what he has called the 'ancient, cold, explosive, detonating impartiality' of the Irish mind.[77] Literature in Yeats is the forgiveness of sins, but it is also 'a portion of the conscience of mankind.'[78] Perhaps the Young Man succeeds for a moment, like Yeats in *A Vision*, in holding 'in a single thought reality and justice,'[79] the reality of Diarmuid and Dervorgilla's tragedy and its justice. 'All art,' Yeats says elsewhere, 'is the disengaging of a soul from place and history, its suspension in a beautiful or terrible light to await the Judgment, though it must be, seeing that all its days were a Last Day, judged already.'[80] He speaks of John Synge as 'one of those unmoved souls in whom there is a perpetual "Last Day," a perpetual trumpeting and coming up for judgment.'[81] We can say that the Young Man, though he has been deeply responsive to Diarmuid and Dervorgilla's love and suffering, has achieved being one of those unmoved souls. But he has achieved it not just by refusing forgiveness. He has achieved it by his full imagination of their situation, by his passing beyond narrow abstraction to tragic awareness. 'How can one, if one's mind be full of abstractions and images created not for their own sake but for the sake of party [Yeats asks his fellow writers] ... make pictures for the mind's eye and sounds that delight the ear, or discover thoughts that tighten the muscles, or quiver and tingle in the flesh, and so stand like Saint Michael with the trumpet that calls the body to resurrection?'[82]

Yeats's purpose in writing *The Dreaming of the Bones*, or at least the point of view which he felt it expressed, was narrow enough: 'The point of view is,' he wrote to Stephen Gwynn on 18 October 1918, that 'England once ... treated Ireland as Germany treated Belgium.'[83] He does not go on to ask, but the question is implicit, if England once treated Ireland as Germany treated Belgium, why should Ireland or Irishmen forgive the English wrongs, refrain from revolutionary activity, or support England in the war with Germany? In the situation, the temptation to forgive Diarmuid and Dervorgilla can only be equated with the temptation to forgive the disastrous involvement of Ireland with England through a long history. The Young Man refuses that forgiveness, and the lesson is that Irishmen should

Arlene Mlodzik as The Morrigu

Kevin McGarrigle as Emer

make the same refusal. Yeats wrote to Lady Gregory that the play is 'I am afraid only too powerful politically'[84] and to Gwynn that the play 'may be thought dangerous by your editor because of its relation to rising of 1916.'[85] Professor Roger McHugh has rightly said that 'to consider this dreamy, impressionistic, and obscure little play about the cyclic involvements of history as being politically powerful is probably quite unreal.'[86] I think it should also be said that the play's political message is placed so clearly in the context of ultimate human tragedy that that message is quite dwarfed and subordinated. It is not the lack of forgiveness, but the cost of the lack of forgiveness, however just, which is dramatised.

Hic and Ille: Shaw and Yeats

M. J. SIDNELL

Bernard Shaw is not the first playwright who comes to mind in connection with the Abbey Theatre – and it may be as a consequence that W. B. Yeats is. In the early history of the Abbey, Shaw is a tangential figure and in the history of Bernard Shaw the Abbey is no less peripheral.

The conjunction of Shaw and the Abbey before 1916 left no visible impression on the artistic life of the theatre. *The Shewing Up of Blanco Posnet* was produced in 1909 as a political act and its production was a political victory over the Lord Chamberlain in England and his unconstitutional counterparts in Dublin. The defeat of the Castle authorities by Yeats and the Abbey was more perfect than that of the English censorship by Bernard Shaw: 'The statement that you bowdlerised the play,' wrote Shaw to Yeats, 'practically confesses that it is not fit for representation.'[1] That the victory was unequally shared between them is in keeping with the Yeats-Shaw relationship, just as it is that the first performance of a play by Shaw arose out of a political and not a literary alliance. It is also in keeping with the general pattern that the play should be a parody of an American 'western' so utterly devoid of Irish matter as to suggest a rather ghostly silence.

The ghosts behind the silence are the attempts that Yeats and Shaw had made, never at the same moment or with the same play, to introduce Shaw into the Irish dramatic movement. Of these attempts the most important, but not the first, occurred in 1904.

In December of that year, Yeats and Lady Gregory with the support of Miss Horniman opened the Abbey Theatre and some months earlier, Shaw had offered Yeats and his company a play that they could have produced for the inauguration. That Bernard Shaw did *not* become the first Abbey playwright was no doubt a non-event with consequences for literary and possibly even political developments in Ireland. And the initial rejection of his *John Bull's Other Island* by the Abbey-to-be may even be a matter for rejoicing. One certainly cannot fancifully substitute for that chapter called 'Yeats and the Abbey' in a hypothetical history of modern Irish literature one called 'Bernard Shaw and the Abbey' without re-imagining that whole history. But my purpose is not speculation about what did not happen. What I propose is the presentation of parts of some unpublished letters from Yeats to Shaw and, by placing them in the context of the familiar and by supplying connectives, to let Yeats and Shaw illuminate their personal and literary relationship. And in particular to direct attention to some of the issues bearing on the rejection of *John Bull's Other Island*.

Yeats's first meeting with Shaw took place at one of William Morris's evenings early in 1888 when Shaw was thirty-one and Yeats nine years younger. The younger man's assessment of his senior was that Shaw had wit rather than humour and a mind 'wanting in depth.'[2] Yeats did not change this basic view throughout the half-century of their acquaintance though he was to qualify it in some immensely important ways. When, in 1932, Yeats was involved in 'impassioned debate' over the founding of an Irish Academy of Letters – his own idea – the occasion was one of those on which the election or rejection of individual men would convey a sense of values.[3] The list of the names of founding members would be a commentary on Ireland's past and a declaration of intention for Ireland's future.

Yeats chose Shaw (who was in England) as his ally in laying the foundations of the Academy while he himself attended to the active business of persuasion, and Yeats succeeded in persuading the steering committee to elect nearly all his own candidates (even St John Ervine, by waiting till the others had gone home) including Shaw as president. It was no idle tribute that Yeats paid to Shaw on that occasion and certainly no merely political gesture. Six years before he had tried to persuade the Royal Irish Academy to create an autonomous literary section and Shaw's name had been the first on his list of prospective members at that time. Many years before that, Yeats had discovered that Shaw, 'the notorious hater of romance' as he at first saw him, the man who had haunted him in nightmare as a smiling sewing-machine, was also generous and courageous to an extent that he had not at first fathomed.[4] Shaw for his part had from the first recognised and endorsed Yeats's claim to greatness.

The foundation of the relationship was properly laid in 1894. They already had a good deal in common, their art, Morris, Wilde, and their circles and their Irish upbringing, and to the links that bound them were now added their joint début in the commercial theatre and two women. Miss Horniman – that ubiquitous, anonymous, can-tankerous, and withal discriminating 'angel' – was one of them and she had given financial backing to the other woman to produce some new plays. Florence Farr, the other woman, asked Yeats to write a play and Shaw gave her, in a difficult moment, his *Arms and the Man*. Both playwrights enjoyed bicycle rides and love affairs with her, though not, I believe, in that same season and in Yeats's case only briefly. The season according to Shaw was something of a flop but later, as he observed, it wore a different complexion. Miss Horniman emerged as the 'original discoverer of the great GBS' (Shaw's words) and also of W. B. Yeats, playwright; and she continued to back Shaw's plays, as well as Yeats's theatre. (Both playwrights incidentally took some time to discover Miss Horniman. One of them with great psychic power penetrated her anonymity in a dream – and that one was

Shaw.) Some five years later Florence Farr was to help Yeats inaugur-
ate the Irish Literary Theatre and later still joined him in the experiments in cantilation – futile nonsense according to Shaw that would
serve to 'intensify ordinary twaddling into a nerve destroying crooning
like the maunderings of an idiot-banshee.'[5]

With his usual good taste, Shaw saw Yeats the playwright as a
'genuine discovery' and thought the *Land of Heart's Desire* 'exquis-
ite.'[6] Yeats, though mostly preoccupied with his own short play –
seeing it night after night – listened to *Arms and the Man* with admiration for the play's energy and for the way in which Shaw tricked an
unfriendly audience into laughing at themselves when they thought
at first that they were laughing at the playwright. And he listened
with hatred for the play's 'inorganic, logical straightness', its lack of
music, style, and emotion.[7] But Yeats's deeper response was not to
Shaw's play but to Shaw himself: Shaw dealing with the audience
from the stage during and after the performance became for Yeats
at that moment 'the most formidable man in modern letters. ... He
could hit my enemies and the enemies of all I loved as I could never
hit, as no living author that was dear to me could ever hit.'[8] A few
years later Yeats was hitting Shaw in debate and proving according
to his own account 'that Shaw's point of view belonged to a bygone
generation – to the scientific epoch – and was now "reactionary." I
think I beat him,' adds Yeats and then, modestly, 'He was not in very
good form, however.'[9] In subsequent battles with others, the issues
were to be more vital and Yeats continually demonstrated that he had
learned well from Shaw and became himself no less formidable than
the master. As for Shaw, he went on immediately after *Arms and the
Man* to write his play about the love of a mature socialist and an im-
mature poet for the same candid woman.

In 1901 with the Irish Literary Theatre well launched and Dublin
already stirring, Yeats asked Shaw to come to Ireland and help 'stir
things up still further.' Yeats had neglected Shaw's suggestion that
The Devil's Disciple might be performed in Dublin. 'It was the very

play for this country,' wrote Yeats, 'as indeed you said to me – but I did not understand.'

The recognition of Shaw's ability to stir things up in a profitable way is characteristic, but the comment on Shaw's play is not. This new and short-lived enthusiasm for Shaw's work arises apparently from the Irish response to the end of *The Man of Destiny*:

Some of the young men of the Extreme National Party are reading you just now with great satisfaction. 'The United Irishman' had a long quotation from your 'Napoleon' about English character a few weeks ago. They would welcome you over with enthusiasm.

That both Yeats and the extreme nationalists would welcome Shaw seems, in the light of subsequent events, to arise from Shaw's adopton of an Irish point of view without, mercifully, talking about Ireland.

The passage Yeats refers to is the finale to *The Man of Destiny* in which Napoleon tells the half-Irish and therefore intelligent heroine who is also half-English and therefore unscrupulous that:

No Englishman is too low to have scruples: no Englishman is high enough to be free from their tyranny. ... When he wants a thing, he never tells himself that he wants it. He waits patiently until there comes into his mind, no one knows how, a burning conviction that it is his moral and religious duty to conquer those who possess the thing he wants. Then he becomes irresistible. He is never at a loss for an effective moral attitude. As the great champion of freedom and national independence, he conquers and annexes half the world. ... When he wants a new market for his adulterated Manchester goods, he sends a missionary to teach the natives the Gospel of Peace. The natives kill the missionary: he flies to arms in defence of Christianity; fights for it; conquers for it and takes the market as a reward from heaven.[10]

This might be 'inorganic logical straightness,' but the sentiments could not be more dear. Like Swift, Shaw was to be most useful and dear to Ireland when addressing England or at least seeing Ireland in its rela-tion to England.

Shaw did not come to Dublin and he did not want the Irish Literary Theatre to do *The Man of Destiny* where his attack on the English and his praise of the Irish would lose their critical point, for the play is of course addressed to an English audience. Instead he agreed to write a play especially for Yeats's theatre and an Irish audience. According to Shaw :

John Bull's Other Island was written in 1904 at the request of Mr William Butler Yeats, as a patriotic contribution to the repertory of the Irish Liter-ary Theatre. Like most people who have asked me to write plays, Mr Yeats got rather more than he bargained for. The play was at that time beyond the resources of the new Abbey Theatre ... [11]

The irony of that 'patriotic' with its peculiarly Shavian connotations and the ambiguity of 'resources' partly give the game away. It was volunteered rather than requested according to Yeats, but whatever the arrangement Shaw's promise was received by Yeats with great enthusiasm, an enthusiasm that lasted until he read the play. Having read it, Yeats was in a quandary. Here was the opportunity for the Abbey Theatre to launch itself with the work of an internationally known playwright. The play would excite the Dublin audience in ways that no play of Yeats, Synge, or Lady Gregory could. However, the work would be difficult to stage and Yeats disliked it.

When he received a copy of the play Yeats read it and gave it to Synge and to William Fay for their opinions before replying to Shaw. Fay's response was that it was :

a wonderful piece of work. But as to our using it I would like a longer time to consider it. ... It is full of fine things but the difficulty of getting a cast for it would be considerable. I don't know how [Shaw] expects to get a show of it in London for with the exception of the Englishman and his valet the rest would have to be Irish born and bred to get the hang of what he wants.[12]

Synge thought some cuts necessary and Yeats in replying to Shaw made much of the need for cutting. I quote part of Yeats's long letter:

I was disappointed by the first act and a half. The stage Irishman who wasn't an Irishman was very amusing but then I said to myself 'What the devil did Shaw mean by all this Union of Hearts-like conversation? What do we care here in this country, which despite the Act of Union is still an island, about the English liberal party and the Tariff, and the difference between English and Irish character, or whatever else it was all about? Being raw people,' I said, 'we do care about human nature in action, and that he's not giving us.'

The Irish interest in descriptions of national character which had waxed so strong with *The Man of Destiny* is now on the wane as Shaw's bright sun rises over Ireland:

No debauchery that ever coarsened and brutalised an Englishman can take the worth and usefulness out of him like that dreaming. An Irishman's imagination never lets him alone, never convinces him, never satisfies him; but it makes him that he can't face reality nor deal with it nor handle it nor conquer it: he can only sneer at them that do. He can't be religious. The inspired Churchman that teaches him the sanctity of life and the importance of conduct is sent away empty; while the poor village priest that gives him a miracle or a sentimental story of a saint, has cathedrals built for him out of the pennies of the poor. He can't be intelligently political: he dreams of what the Shan Van Vocht said in ninetyeight. If you want to interest him in Ireland you've got to call the unfortunate island Kathleen ni Hollihan and pretend she's a little old woman. It saves thinking. It saves working.[13]

So says Shaw's Doyle, one of the real Irishmen in the play. That reference to 'raw people' – an uncharacteristic phrase to come from Yeats at this time – seems to be an adjustment of his attitude to the Irish people which will make possible a better defensive stance from which to respond to this kind of description of an Irish peasant:

The real tragedy of Haffigan is the tragedy of his wasted youth, his stunted mind, his drudging over his clods and pigs until he has become a clod and a pig himself – until the soul within him has smouldered into nothing but a dull temper that hurts himself and all around him. I say let him die, and let us have no more of his like.[14]

Yeats continues his critique, finding more to praise, balancing his respect for Shaw's sense of comedy and intelligent concern for Ireland against that logical straightness he hated:

Then my interest began to awake. That young woman who persuaded that Englishman, full of impulsiveness that comes from a good banking account, that he was drunk on nothing more serious than poteen, was altogether a delight. The motor car too, the choosing the member of Parliament, and so on right to the end, often exciting and mostly to the point. I thought in reading the first act that you had forgotten Ireland, but I found in the other acts that is the only subject on which you are entirely serious. In fact you are so serious that sometimes your seriousness leaps upon the stage, knocks the characters over, and insists on having all the conversation to himself. However the inevitable cutting (the play is as you say immensely too long) is certain to send your seriousness back to the front row of the stalls. You have said things in this play which are entirely true about Ireland, things which nobody has ever said before, and these are the very things that are most part of the action. It astonishes me that you should have been so long in London and yet have remembered so much. To some extent this play is unlike anything you have done before. Hitherto you have taken your situations from melodrama, and called up logic to make them ridiculous. Your process here seems to be quite different, you are taking your situations more from life, you are for the first time trying to get the atmosphere of a place, you have for the first time a geographical conscience. (For instance you have not made the landlords the winning side, as you did the Servians in the first version of *Arms and the Man.*)

The criticism is not so much a view of the whole work as a record of Yeats's changing impressions as the play unfolded for him : a tribute to its author's sheepdog skill in herding his audience. And Yeats's response is not unlike in kind, though different in quality, that description of the way in which the boobies who had gone to disrupt *Arms and the Man* fell into Shaw's trap. Yeats steers clear of Shaw's professional Irishman handily enough, but is irritated and confused by the sentimental English celticist and the really Irish internationalist, as he was meant to be. Shaw's Doyle deplores his father's ambition 'to make St George's Channel a frontier and hoist a flag on College Green'. 'Ireland,' insists Yeats, 'is still an island.' Having expended his energy reacting to the early part of the play Yeats is softened for indoctrination by Shaw with new and, he acknowledges, true comments on Ireland.

In his 'Preface for Politicians,' Shaw later put succinctly the attitude to nationalism that permeates *John Bull's Other Island* :

The great movements of the human spirit which sweep in waves over Europe are stopped on the Irish coast by the English guns of the Pigeon House Fort. Only a quaint little offshoot of English pre-Raphaelitism called the Gaelic movement has got a footing by using Nationalism as a stalking-horse, and popularising itself as an attack on the native language of the Irish people, which is most fortunately also the native language of half the world, including England.[15]

Shaw's blow is shrewdly aimed at Yeats. Far from being a poet drawing strength from the native culture, Yeats is implicitly characterised as one bamboozled by a sentimental, affected, and effete primitivism. In sharing a platform with the Gaelic League Yeats saw himself authenticating his Irishness but Shaw, who had little interest in sharing platforms, demolishes the one that Yeats had laboured to construct.

Perhaps Yeats's unfavourable comment on the first part of the play, and the impudent comment on cutting that I am about to read, indicate that he would have liked to present the latter part of the play in Dublin:

I asked him [Synge] to make suggestions about cuts, as I thought that our knowledge of local interests here might be valuable to you. I shall myself have one or two suggestions on details to make, but they can stand over. I have no doubt you will cut in your own way, but you may as well hear them. I had a theory when I was a boy that a play should be very long, and contain a great deal about everything, put in quite without respect to times and occasions, and that every man who played it should take the slice that suited him. I cannot say I hold that theory now, but there is something in it, the two parts of Goethe's *Faust* for instance, and the use all sorts of people make of them. To my surprise I must say, I do not consider the play dangerous. There may be a phrase, but I cannot think of one at this moment. Here again, you show your wonderful knowledge of the country. You have laughed at all the things that are ripe for laughter, and not where the ear is still green. I don't mean to say that there won't be indignation about one thing or another, and a great deal of talk about it all, but I mean that we can play it, and survive to play something else.

The comment on Shaw's dramaturgy is impudently put, but is not without foundation. Yeats had indeed started with a five-act structure derived from Elizabethan models and had moved towards a new conception of dramatic form. Shaw, on the other hand, retained and revitalised the traditional model of the 'well-made play.' The question of survival did not arise. The play was not played at the Abbey – that is not until 1916.

On Shaw's side there had clearly been no dependence on a Dublin performance and before he had sent the play to Yeats he was already planning the London opening.[16] Indeed one suspects that Shaw's 'patriotic contribution' was designed for performance in London and for rejection by the Irish National Theatre Company; and, moreover, that it was made with a lively interest in embarrassing and educating Yeats. In the event, *John Bull's Other Island* inaugurated the Vedrenne-Barker productions with great éclat. Yeats saw this English production and took note of the acclamation. As though to pass over a distasteful matter as quickly as possible, he wrote to Lady Gregory:

I have seen Shaw's play; it acts very much better than one could have foreseen, but it is immensely long. It begins at 2.30 and ends at 6. I don't really like it. It is fundamentally ugly and shapeless, but certainly keeps everybody amused.[17]

John Bull's Other Island is the headiest mixture of paradoxical wit that Shaw concocted: the dramatic conceit is extended to the last possible degree of characterisation and action. Doyle, the Shavian Irishman, is set off against professional Irishmen, English celticists, reactionary catholics, the Irish peasant landlord who is stupider, more grasping, and a greater obstacle to material progress than the English absentee kind, and all those who, in an Irish context, obstruct the Life Force. Shaw was certainly not wholly wrong in saying, as he did later, that the play 'was uncongenial to the whole spirit of the neo-Gaelic movement, which is bent on creating a new Ireland after its own ideal, whereas my play is a very uncompromising presentment of the real old Ireland.'[18]

That Shaw's portrait of the 'real old Ireland' might be scandalous libel is scarcely to the point. The portraiture is caricature, existing for the sake of the criticism of Irish life it embodies. Through his Doyle Shaw gives us the view of an internationalist in the forefront of the evolutionary process that the Life Force is unfolding :

Now whatever else metallurgical chemistry may be it's not national. It's international. And my business and yours as civil engineers is to join countries, not to separate them. The one real political conviction that our business has rubbed into us is that frontiers are hindrances and flags confounded nuisances.[19]

Through Doyle, Ireland is contained within the Shavian scheme of creative evolution, the linear process described so elaborately in *Back to Methuselah* that begins with individuality and carnality in fallen Eden, passes through socialism, internationalism, and technology in civilisation, and ends in the realms of pure incorporeal thought in the last part of the Pentateuch : the very antithesis of the Yeatsian vision of essential individuality, of morality manifested through race, of re-currence and reincarnation, of the eternal opposition of spirit and body, and of sexuality that tries and fails to bridge the gulf.

In 1937, when Yeats was doing battle with the British over the forged Casement diaries and Shaw wrote a 'long, rambling' letter urging Irishmen not to stir up strife between the nations, it was not loosely that Yeats called the letter 'sexless' for the national contraries were, metaphorically at least, sexual and so productive.[20] Here as elsewhere he was commenting on the logical, straight, and single-stranded character of Shaw's thought which contrasted so violently with the fecund duality of his own.

But, as I have said, it is the logical Doyle in *John Bull's Other Island* who gives us the characteristically Shavian view, and Doyle's views do not in the end utterly prevail. In the play's final paradox Doyle meets a man who is at least his equal : Keegan, the loony, unfrocked priest. From Keegan we hear that 'Every dream is a prophecy : every jest is an earnest in the womb of Time,' and this Irish dreamer, self-confessed madman, and poet leaves the efficient Shavian economist standing. Perhaps it is here, through the medium of fiction, in the last act of *John Bull's Other Island*, that we have the most telling account of the Shaw-Yeats relationship as it might have appeared to Shaw; or, if we accept fictional accounts (and Shaw's insistence that his writing was confessional), then one may find a kind of a Shaw and a sort of Yeats (and maybe a Florence Farr, too) in *Candida*. In Keegan of *John Bull's Other Island*, in Eugene Marchbanks of *Candida* one may see their creator's astonishment, irritation, and admiration for poets and dreamers like Yeats; in Doyle and Morell, one sees the self-caricature of Shavianism, the heroic moral and intellectual struggle, the final defeat by a poetry that is superior, despite its ludicrous aspects. At the end of *Candida*, Morell is in secure possession of his wife, but Eugene Marchbanks, the poet and rival (who unaccountably has bits of heather sticking to his suit), goes off with a splendid secret in his heart which Morell and Candida do not know, and which, whatever the details, is clearly a superior vision.

At the end of *John Bull's Other Island* the unfrocked priest presents a vision of an Ireland run on good economic principles, well-fed, prosperous, and thoroughly efficient in every way, and it is a vision of Ireland betrayed by Irishmen and of Hell. Then he marches off to his Round Tower to dream of eternity, having demonstrated Doyle's idea of progress to be a half-truth at the best and leaving Doyle looking like a 'stillborn poet.'

The play finally acknowledges its own inappropriateness as a contribution to the creation of new moral and national purpose. For Edwardian England Shaw's emetic irony was salutary. Dublin in 1904, according to the best testimony for that year, Joyce's farraginous chronicle, stood more in need of unifying vision than analytical criticism: more in need of creative image than the intellectual structure erected by Shaw as a gallery in which to hang caricatures of the folly of his time.

The fundamental issue between Yeats and Shaw was not political necessity or artistic independence : it was the distinction made in 'Ego Dominus Tuus' between Hic and Ille, whose names for the moment I take the liberty of changing :

YEATS By the help of my own image
   I call to my own opposite, summon all
   That I have handled least, least looked upon.
SHAW And I would find myself and not an image.
YEATS That is our modern hope, and by its light
   We have lit upon the gentle, sensitive mind
   And lost the old nonchalance of the hand;
   Whether we have chosen chisel, pen or brush
   We are but critics, or but half create ...
   The struggle of the fly in marmalade.
   The rhetorician would deceive his neighbours
   The sentimentalist himself; while art
   Is but a vision of reality ...
SHAW Why should you leave the lamp
   Burning alone beside an open book,
   And trace these characters upon the sands?
   A style is found by sedentary toil
   And by the imitation of great masters.
YEATS Because I seek an image, not a book.

Perhaps the dialogue would be more evenly balanced if the Yeats/Ille part only were taken from this poem and the Shaw/Hic part from Pope's 'Essay on Criticism.' For the argument is at bottom between those canons we call classical and can define, and that view we call romantic and cannot; and though patriotism may belong to both, nationalism seems to be an aspect of the latter only. And in this respect particularly, there is a difference between the work of Shaw on the one hand and that of O'Casey and Yeats on the other. Nationalism in Shaw is neither higher nor lower, but absent.

In the seond version of *A Vision* Yeats illustrated his commentary on the 'Twenty-Eight Incarnations' with examples of particular people, most of them drawn from the ranks of the long dead. Under Phase 21 three contemporaries are cited as examples: Shaw, H. G. Wells, and George Moore. Part of Yeats's description of men of this phase seems not so much to apply to, as to be drawn from the model of, Bernard Shaw in particular:

He apprehends ... some vast systemisation, in which the will imposes itself upon the multiplicity of living images, or events, upon all in Shake-speare, in Napoleon even, that delighted in its independent life; for he is a tyrant and must kill his adversary. If he is a novelist, his characters must go his road, and not theirs, and perpetually demonstrate his thesis; he will love construction better than the flow of life, and as a dramatist he will create character and situation without passion, and without liking, and yet he is a master of surprise, for one can never be sure where even a charge of shot will fall. Style exists now but as a sign of work well done, a certain energy and precision of movement; in an artistic sense it is no longer possible, for the tension of the will is too great to allow of sug-gestion. Writers of the phase are great public men and they exist after death as historical monuments, for they are without meaning apart from time and circumstance.[21]

With the essence of this view, Shaw, whose bragging and pontificating did not conceal his real modesty, did not disagree. Despite his attacks on Shakespeare (which were often attacks on bardolatry) Shaw had the wit to recognise that *A Midsummer Night's Dream* would still be as fresh as paint when much of his own work would be as flat as ditchwater – though of course he insisted that his plays would have been of more use than those of Shakespeare.

And here, I believe, lies the reason for the mutual admiration and respect that survived in Shaw and Yeats despite their contrary views and such incidents as the rejection of *John Bull's Other Island*. Both men recognised in Yeats the enduring poet with a vision of eternity, both men recognised in Shaw a great public man to whom his contemporaries were much indebted for the scourge of his wit; and both men recognised themselves as complementary figures, two lines of descent it might be, from a common ancestor, Jonathan Swift.

SEVEN LETTERS FROM W. B. YEATS TO BERNARD SHAW*

[These letters are part of MS50553 of the Shaw papers in the British Museum. They are published here by the kind permission of Senator Michael B. Yeats. Yeats's minor corrections to the texts have been incorporated silently and in those taken from typescripts the typist's errors are also corrected. The punctuation and spelling have been conventionalised, the former with as little interference as possible with the text. 'Sincerely' and 'ever' in the final signature are not often legible and I have sometimes guessed at the more likely word by its length.]

Letter One

[1 folded sheet of 'Coole Park' letterhead. Holograph.]

at
Coole Park,
Gort
Co. Galway

Oct 1901

My Dear Shaw : I write to urge you to come over and see our 'Theatre' this year. You will find all that is stormy in Dublin gathered and feathered – and Dublin is full of stir just now – and we will set you to speak, if you

* © Michael B. Yeats

will be so good. Come over and help us stir things up still further. Both Lady Gregory – with whom I am staying – & myself are regretting that we did not try and get 'The Devil's Disciple' from you for our Theatre. It was the very play for this country – as indeed you said to me – but I did not understand.

Some of the young men of the Extreme National party are reading you just now with great satisfaction. 'The United Irishman' had a long quotation from your 'Napoleon' about English character a few weeks ago. They would welcome you over with enthusiasm.

Yours ever

W. B. Yeats

Letter Two

[Two sheets. Typescript done by Lady Gregory's typewriter, I believe, with corrections in Yeats's hand.]

Coole Park
Gort, Co Galway

Oct. 5 1904

My Dear Shaw : I have been very long about thanking you for the play. I waited until I could give you Fay's opinion and Synge's. I sent the play to Synge the moment I had read it, and he went off to Belmullet, and neither wrote nor sent an address until yesterday. He sent the play back however through a member of the company he met on the way to Belmullet, and I sent it to William Fay, from whom I have heard this morning. I enclose his letter. Synge who is always rather languid in his letter writing tells me very little, except that he will tell me a great deal when we meet next week at rehearsal. Now as to my own opinion.

I was disappointed by the first act and a half. The stage Irishman who wasn't an Irishman was very amusing, but then I said to myself 'What the devil did Shaw mean by all this Union of Hearts-like Conversation?

What do we care here in this country, which despite the Act of Union is still an island, about the English liberal party and the Tariff, and the difference between English and Irish character, or whatever else it was all about. Being raw people,' I said, 'we do care about human nature in action, and that he's not giving us.' Then my interest began to awake. That young woman who persuaded that Englishman, full of impulsiveness that comes from a good banking account, that he was drunk on nothing more serious than poteen, was altogether a delight. The motor car too, the choosing the member of Parliament, and so on right to the end, often exciting and mostly to the point. I thought in reading the first act that you had forgotten Ireland, but I found in the other acts that is the only subject on which you are entirely serious. In fact you are so serious that sometimes your seriousness leaps upon the stage, knocks the characters over, and insists on having all the conversation to himself. However the inevitable cutting (the play is as you say immensely too long) is certain to send your seriousness back to the front row of the stalls. You have said things in this play which are entirely true about Ireland, things which nobody has ever said before, and these are the very things that are most part of the action. It astonishes me that you should have been so long in London and yet have remembered so much. To some extent this play is unlike anything you have done before. Hitherto you have taken your situations from melodrama, and called up logic to make them ridiculous. Your process here seems to be quite different, you are taking your situations more from life, you are for the first time trying to get the atmosphere of a place, you have for the first time a geographical conscience. (For instance you have not made the landlords the winning side, as you did the Servians in the first version of *Arms and the Man*.)

Synge who is as good an opinion as I know, thinks that 'it will hold a Dublin audience, and at times move them if even tolerably played.' He thinks however you should cut the Grasshopper, and a scene which I cannot recall, but which he describes as 'the Handy Andy-like scene about carrying the goose' and some of the Englishman's talk about Free Trade, Tariffs, etc. I asked him to make suggestions about cuts, as I thought that our knowledge of local interests here might be valuable to you. I shall myself have one or two suggestions on details to make, but they can stand over. I have no doubt you will cut in your own way, but you may as well hear them. I had a theory when I was a boy that a play should be very long, and contain a great deal about everything, put in quite without respect to times and occasions, and that every man who played it should take the slice that suited him. I cannot say I hold that theory now, but there is something in it, the two parts of Goethe's *Faust* for instance, and the use all sorts of people make of them. To my surprise I must say, I do not consider the play dangerous. There may be a phrase, but I cannot think of one at this moment. Here again, you show your wonderful knowledge of the country. You have laughed at all the things that are ripe for laughter, and not where the ear is still green. I don't mean to say that there won't be indignation about one thing or another, and a great deal of talk about it all, but I mean that we can play it, and survive to play something else. You will see by Fay's letter that he is nervous about being able to cast it. I imagine the Englishman will give us most difficulty, but it will all be difficult.

I shall be in Dublin next week, and will talk the whole matter over with the company. It would be a help if you could let me know your own feeling about cuts. I will then have the play in my hands again and can go into detail.

Yours sincerely

W. B. Yeats

Letter Three

[One sheet. Holograph. The reference to difficulties with Miss Horniman and to Mrs Lyttelton's involvement make 1909 the almost indubitable year of writing, the unnamed play *The Shewing Up of Blanco Posnet* and the month July or August. By the last week of August Shaw was in Ireland, though he declined to leave Kerry for Dublin to join the *Blanco Posnet* battle in person.]

C/O Lady Gregory
Burren
Co Clare

[July or August 1909]

Dear Shaw : Let me know if you are coming over to rehearse, as if not other arrangements must be made, and if we are to have the parts typed or if you can send us copies. It takes a little time getting the parts ready.

Miss Horniman is quiet just now but I thought she was going to bring us to an end. She would have done so but for Mrs Lyttelton.
Y. sincerely
W. B. Yeats

Letter Four

[One sheet of Shaw's letterhead paper. Holograph. The references to the negotiations over *O'Flaherty V.C.* are very strong evidence for the date November 1915. A postcard from Shaw apparently answering the letter below is dated 14 Nov. 1915. Shaw insists on no cuts for licensing purposes and sends a duplicate of his card to Dublin in response to Yeats's final comment, no doubt.]

10 Adelphi Terrace

[13 or 14 November 1915]

My dear Shaw : I have just seen our agents. The Coliseum see no difficulty about 'O'Flaherty.' They suggest a few slight cuts and apart from that say the play is too long – should play for 30 minutes. I leave you the marked copy (which agents want back as it is their only copy). It may be useful to you with Nathan or the like. I have written to Bailey to say that we should, if military do not give way, give a private performance inviting all Dublin notables & taking up a collection. I may have to go to Dublin tonight.
Yours sincerely
W. B. Yeats

McLeod says no theatre here would object to the play.

[The play was not given at this time. Sir Matthew Nathan wrote a civil and friendly letter to Shaw suggesting that the production should be postponed and W. F. Bailey, Yeats's friend at the Castle, was inclined to agree, as it might be construed as an attack on the actual Mr O'Leary v.c. The following letter refers to the threat of closing the theatre initiated by the military authorities in the interests of their recruiting campaign. This threat seems to have been the deciding factor against production.]

Letter Five

[One sheet of Yeats's letterhead paper. Holograph. The envelope is postmarked with the date 16 Nov. 1915.]

18 Woburn Buildings
W.C.

Monday 16 November 1915

My Dear Shaw : I enclose Bailey's last letter. I see the military authorities did take action or rather threatened action so that the first impression was right. I cannot go to Dublin. I have spent the day in bed with asthmatic attack and bad cold but hope to be able to go out to morrow. However Bailey will manage all right and better than I could in his new mood.
Yours
W. B. Yeats

Letter Six

[One sheet of Yeats's letterhead paper. Typescript]

42 Fitzwilliam Square
Dublin
Phone 61831

April 26 1932

My Dear Shaw : I have deposited the fifty pounds in the Bank of Ireland
in the name of the Irish Academy of Letters and have ordered a rubber
stamp —. Today I had an interview with the Abbey lawyer and was
advised to register the Academy under the Friendly Societies Act, and
to seek no further publicity until registration had taken place. If we regis-
tered under the Companies Act we should have to apply to the Executive
Council for leave to omit the word 'Limited,' and it seems undesir-
able to draw attention to ourselves at present. I return to Coole Park
tomorrow and shall be there until May 12th. I hope that while I am away
Starkie, George Russell, and Frank O'Connor will draft a set of rules,
the minimum necessary for registration. I think that is all I have to report
for the present.

Yours sincerely, W. B. Yeats

[For the context of this letter and the one below see *The Letters of
W. B. Yeats*, ed. Allan Wade (London 1954), 800 *et seq*]

Letter Seven

[Two typescript sheets with MS corrections. Yeats's letterhead paper
with the address '42 Fitzwilliam Square' has been used with this
printed address deleted and the one given below substituted in Yeats's
hand.]

Riversdale
Willbrook
Rathfarnham, Dublin

September 15 1932

My Dear Shaw : We held our first meeting of the provisional council last
night, it lasted for four hours and was so impassioned that nobody went

out to look at the eclipse. It began by a general insistence that they should all have nomination papers, that such a document with your signature to it was an heirloom, or something of that kind, further that those who had already accepted but were not present should have nomination papers; then somebody said 'I think Shaw and Yeats should have nomination papers.' Then we elected you president and settled down to our impassioned debate. Though you and I are nominating we are working under The Friendly Societies Act which requires that those we nominate should be voted by the provisional committee. The council was not at all docile, every name was debated, sometimes friendly, but I got finally the list I wanted except that I had for the present to abandon the Blasket Islander. I found that St John Ervine was universally hated but I got him through when the majority of the committee had gone home (there will be trouble when they find out). The opposition to him arose when it was discovered that we had too many on the list; I managed however to substitute him for the Blasket Islander. I send you the new forms to be filled up. Amongst them you will find two or three names that I had forgotten (have I already sent you a form for L. A. G. Strong? I mean, since I sent the main list?) And there is one new name, wanted passionately by the majority of the provisional council, Sean O'Faolain; he is the author of 'Midsummer Madness,' a book greatly commended by Edward Garnet. He fought on the Republican side and has put his experience into the book. It is a crude, ugly, powerful book.

I lecture at 'The Peacock Theatre,' a little experimental theatre connected with the Abbey and under the same roof, on Sunday night for the benefit of the Academy. The list of members, etc. will be given to the press at my lecture.

Yours ever, W. B. Yeats

[The 'Blasket Islander' is probably Tomás Crithin, author of *An t Oileánach* (*The Islandman,* 1929), but possibly Muiris Ó Súileabháin, author of *Fiche Blian ag Fás* (*Twenty Years A-growing* 1933).]

The absence of nationalism in the work of Samuel Beckett

FRANCIS WARNER

It is my pleasure, in this seminar on theatre and nationalism in twentieth-century Ireland, to give this final lecture, as an Englishman, on the absence of nationalism in the theatre of Samuel Beckett. And after such tales as we have heard of heroism and self-sacrifice we may care to recall that Mr Beckett, too, in his earlier days received a knife through his body; but his assailant alas was not English but a Frenchman, and the cause a rather less romantic one, so the attacker told him when Beckett visited him in gaol, not nationalism but whim.

Beckett, indeed left Ireland for Paris in October 1928, and although he has made various return visits to his native country, has made Paris and the Marne district his home ever since. Influenced by James Joyce, his early mentor during these days, he decided that exile was appropriate for him also, and having tried the life of a don at Trinity chose to abdicate his scholastic ambitions and make his home abroad. As Mrs Rooney remarks in *All That Fall*: 'It is suicide to be abroad. But what is it to be at home, Mr Tyler, what is it to be at home? A lingering dissolution.'

But although Beckett settled in France, he has not become a Frenchman. We do not think of him, or indeed address him, as M. Beckett. He has kept, studiously up-to-date, his passport. On his walls hang reminders of Ireland, including a beautiful Jack Yeats oil painting of Trinity boathouse on the Liffey.[1] His country cottage overlooks what can only be described as the most Irish stretch of landscape in the whole of the region: 'Glorious prospect, but for the mist that blotted out everything, valleys, loughs, plain and sea.'[2] And when I saw him last he was once again greatly enjoying George Moore's *Hail and Farewell*.

Oscar Wilde once said to Yeats, 'We Irish are too poetical to be poets'; and Beckett might equally answer that he is too Irish to be a nationalist. Certainly he has never rejected Ireland in any save a bodily way, and before him not only Joyce but Shaw, Wilde, Goldsmith, Congreve, and a host of others had done the same. 'I am a typical Irishman,' said Shaw, 'my parents come from Hampshire.' Joyce might have replied 'But I am more typical, Mr Shaw, for my children were born in Trièste.'

Beckett, then, belongs to Ireland and is part of the long tradition that, thanks to many fine scholars such as Vivian Mercier, we know so well. But just how he belongs to it is the subject of my study; and perhaps we should begin by thinking of his relationship with James Joyce before moving back in time and to a wider perspective. James Joyce and Samuel Beckett make each an exactly complementary arc in their lifetime's experiment. They represent contrary but interdependent modes of vision, and each completes the other.

James Joyce wanted to make the soul of the commonest object radiant. He began by writing lyrics that were neo-Elizabethan or post-pre-Raphaelite, graduated to what he called a style of 'scrupulous meanness' for *Dubliners*, began to evolve an organically growing prose style in which form exactly reflected content in *A Portrait of the Artist as a Young Man*; moved on to show his virtuosity with all English and many Gaelic styles in his mistresspiece *Ulysses*, and, his eyes failing, finally brought to birth his 'monster,' *Finnegans Wake*, the most comprehensive and densely-written book ever conceived; revealing in it a style that is at the opposite pole from that of the 'scrupulous meanness' of *Dubliners*. A rich, ever-shifting, punning, holycaust of a book vast in scope and infinite in depth; yet with a recognisable locale, a pub in Dublin on the banks of the Liffey, and a central core of a basic social unit, a family.

Joyce, then, moved from a position of almost Horatian chastity in his approach to language to the most extreme form of baroque – if we take that word to indicate an endlessly complex fantastification round a basically simple function or theme. Joyce progressed from brief and simple to massive and complex, and Beckett has done exactly the opposite.

For his earlier novels are full-length – *Murphy* (1938), *Watt* (1953), *Molloy* (1951). Scene and subject matter narrow in *Malone Dies* (1951), and from then on progressively through *The Unnamable* (1953) (these three last having been written, we should remember, as opposed to published, between 1946 and 1949), the *Texts for Nothing* (1955), and *How It Is* (1961) to *Imagination Dead Imagine* and *Ping*, recently published. So also with the plays; the longer ones such as *Godot* (1952) and *Endgame* (1957) come first, followed by *Krapp's Last Tape* (1959), *Happy Days* (1961), *Play* (1963), and *Come and Go* (1967).

We have to remember that the Beckett who is writing *Come and Go* and *Imagination Dead Imagine* – the shortest play and the shortest novel in our language – is the man who in 1931 with friends published his translation into French of *Anna Livia Plurabelle* (a part of *Finnegans Wake*); and also the following year a prose fragment written in imitation of Joyce's *Work in Progress*[3] seeking on his own account to discover what else might be discovered in the direction of the extreme baroque.

Beckett, then, quite literally, begins where Joyce left off, by translation and imitation of *Finnegans Wake*. The result was the only possible one – a commodius vicus of recirculation back to the utterly simple and plain, which was Joyce's starting-point. Beckett completes the circle begun by Joyce's elliptical experiment: from *Chamber Music* and *Dubliners* to *Finnegans Wake*; from translation and imitation of the *Wake* to *Imagination Dead Imagine* and *Come and Go*.

The outline, then, is clear. But once this has been said, the differences are probably the really important things. Beckett probing the more negative emotions, horror, boredom, the comedy of hopelessness, the problem of speaking when there's nothing to say: and Joyce's gigantic affirmation of life in Molly's 'Yes,' and Kevin's seraphic ardour in his handbathtub and the cry 'Finn no more!' Joyce's problem is rather the putting into a confining straitjacket of words the torrents of an overflowing mind.

Beckett's attitude is in violent contrast. Speaking of Tal Coat in 1949 in the Duthuit dialogues he said :

I speak of an art ... weary of pretending to be able, of being able, of doing a little better the same old thing, of going a little further along a dreary road ... [preferring] the expression that there is nothing to express, nothing with which to express, nothing from which to express, no power to express, no desire to express, together with the obligation to express.

Obviously the attitudes are remote from each other. Nevertheless, the more they are studied, the more the problems of one seem similar to the other's. Clearly Beckett is trying to pare language to the bone, even as his friend Giacometti pared the human form during the same years to its simplest concept, 'the shadow that is cast' and no more.

On the one hand, Joyce in his works is seeking to pack language full of meaning, make 'messes of mottage' many meanings deep, using the ammunition of 'quashed quotatoes' and the setting of the Dublin 'gossipocracy' and its 'slipping beauties.' His challenge is in the very visual form of the word on the dreambookpage. Although much is gained when the *Wake* is read aloud, much also is lost, as Mary Ellen Bute discovered when she filmed parts of it. In the end she very wisely chose to give quotations on the screen under each shot, and by this means considerably enriched the film. Oddly enough, in spite of the enormous musicality of the *Wake*, its full impact must finally be visual, the word on the page.

On the other hand Beckett, working more consciously from the visual arts (we should remember his friendship with artists such as Avigdor Arikha as well as his published criticism on the painting of Jack Yeats and Bram and Geer van Velde), writes a style that, although highly aware visually, does not belong on the written page, but lends itself eminently well to the spoken voice: so much so that he writes dramas, and expects his plays to be seen, acted, or heard on the radio, rather than read. Whereas for Joyce the dreambookpage was the final deliverer, with Beckett the problem of the medium is rather more complex. In *Play* the man on the theatre spotlight is probably of equal importance with those actors whose voices he elicits to articulation, and silences; more especially as in rehearsal Beckett informed him that when the play was repeated for the second act, he could alter the order in which he called the voices from their dark. In *Film* the camera is our surrogate and co-stars with Buster Keaton. The human being perceived was, *Exiles* apart, of no interest to Joyce. For Beckett, at least for the filmscript, *esse est percipi*. But over and above this, in *How It Is* and the *Texts For Nothing* as well as the plays, if there is a final deliverer at all, and this is by no means certain, for him it 'lies' in the human voice.

If this is true, that except in his silent experiments Beckett relies on the human voice to an unmistakable degree, and that voice is also unmistakably Irish, may we not class him as a nationalist?

Artistically we may, as I hope this lecture will demonstrate, but politically we may not, as he 'takes no sides':

I take no sides. I am interested in the shape of ideas. There is a wonderful sentence in Augustine: 'Do not despair; one of the thieves was saved. Do not presume; one of the thieves was damned.' That sentence has a wonderful shape. It is the shape that matters.[4]

You remember how he rephrases this when he writes *Waiting For Godot* : 'One of the thieves was saved. It's a reasonable percentage.' And with this we begin to see how he belongs to that Irish tradition of expatriate and apolitical wits.

Leaving Joyce to one side now, and moving back in time, we may note that the sources of Oscar Wilde's wit (Wilde as you remember with his usual good taste died at the turn of the century in 1900) have several roots, but all depend on the spoken sentence, the conversational tone. When he says 'One's real life is so often the life that one does not lead,' or 'It is perfectly monstrous the way people go about, nowadays, saying things behind one's back that are absolutely and entirely true,' the art lies in part on the shaping tone of voice; and also, in this last, and 'the wages of sin is birth,' what strikes our ear is the substitution of exactly the opposite word for the one we were carefully led to expect. The scene between Lord Goring and his valet Phipps in Act Three of *An Ideal Husband* turns entirely on the common assumption on stage for the moment that the death of a relative is by no means as important as the aesthetic effect of the buttonhole when one is dressing for dinner. In other words, Wilde crosses the technique of comic rhythms of voice with abrupt and startling inversion of expected consequences and values.

Wilde could only do this because of the time in which he lived. Behind him lay the long reign of moral Victoria. Values, at least in public, were clear. He could make his audiences, in theatres and at dinner tables, laugh by leading them on to anticipate the platitude that they themselves would endorse and then turning it inside out. In so doing he acknowledged their morality by so geometrically inverting it.

Beckett it seems can no longer see any system of values stable enough to overturn for his humour. What has happened is that he has taken the forms of diction and dislocated them, in the same way that Wilde took the values of the time and reversed them.

When Beckett writes 'One of the thieves was saved,' he accustoms our ears to the diction of a certain kind of utterance – that of the

Bible, Augustine, the academic, the meditative piety. We do not usually associate such a style of diction with a stockbroker. So the second half of his sentence, 'It's a reasonable percentage,' comes as a shock as we recognise the rhythm in its own right, but from another walk of life so remote that its forced juxtapositioning like this, compelling us to align two classes of value-utterance, makes us laugh at the incongruity.

Again and again this is Beckett's humorous technique; not always to make us laugh, but at times to keep the fractured idiom of dictions present when a laugh is not essential. We remember the comments of the Man in *Play*:

At home all heart to heart, new leaf and bygones bygones. I ran into your ex-doxy, she said one night, on the pillow, you're well out of that. Rather uncalled for, I thought. I am indeed, sweetheart, I said, I am indeed. God what vermin women. Thanks to you, angel, I said.

But consider the later line of Woman 1. 'She had means, I fancy, though she lived like a pig.' No obvious laugh is enjoined, yet middle-class feminine prevarication is immediately coupled with lower-class monosyllabic concrete directness. The art of the verbal unexpected has been taken over from Wilde by Beckett, but transferred from the realm of moral values and common assumptions to the common but amoral assumptions of contemporary speech inflexions.

I take no sides. … That sentence has a wonderful shape. It is the shape that matters.

For Beckett it is also the incongruity of perfectly recognisable dictions.

From Joyce, if we may recall him for a moment, Beckett takes his everpresent love of pun, but it is pun constructed on opposite principles to Joyce's. For Joyce, puns were constructed by combining many meanings and compressing them into one word. Beckett does something rather different. He strips syntax away from a word, leaving it naked and lonely on the page, so that, as the reader supplies many different contexts for the word, it takes on varieties of meaning. Oddly enough, one finds that the more language is stripped, the richer it becomes. His film is called *Film,* and as such this is the generic title. Yet one of the two objects of vision in the film is the camera representing our eyes, and this, at carefully defined moments, blurs, films over, so that we feel our eyes are, in both senses, being filmed.

So it was when he wanted to write a play with no words. The stage direction 'act without words' became the title, and soon by extension in rehearsal, a command. He calls one of his plays after the generic title *Play*; and then in the course of it the Man says 'All this, when will all this have been … just play?' But when we talk of Beckett belonging to the direct line of Anglo-Irish or Dublin Wits, we mean more than the fact that he took the art of moral incongruity and transferred it to the realm of diction, and that he learned from Joyce. Although it is impossible to isolate all that is incorporated by the term Irish Wit, we can note certain aspects that seem to be present, over and above those mentioned, in Beckett, Joyce, and Wilde.

Another is surely the use of imaginative flights upheld over extended metaphors or conceits by their own giddy logic. Wilde in *The Decay of Lying* wrote:

Many a young man starts in life with a natural gift for exaggeration which, if nurtured in congenial and sympathetic surroundings, or by the imitation of the best models, might grow into something really great and wonderful. But, as a rule, he comes to nothing. … He either falls into careless habits of accuracy, or takes to frequenting the society of the aged and the well-informed. Both things are equally fatal to his imagination, as indeed they would be fatal to the imagination of anybody, and in a short time he develops a morbid and unhealthy faculty of truth-telling, begins to verify all statements made in his presence, has no hesitation in contradicting people who are much younger than himself, and often ends by writing novels which are so life-like that no one can possibly believe in their probability.

Here are Wilde's familiar techniques: neatly inverting common assumptions about the wisdom of the old and the health of truth-telling, and pursuing the theme on until it reaches a point which has more than a grain of truth in it. The spectacular flight of irrational fancy is surely one of the marks of the Irish playwrights of this tradition, and one thinks back in time perhaps to Sheridan's Snake in *The School for Scandal*:

LADY SNEERWELL Why, truly, Mrs Clackitt has a very pretty talent and a great deal of industry.

SNAKE True, madam, and has been tolerably successful in her day. To my knowledge, she has been the cause of six matches being broken off, and three sons disinherited; of four forced elopements, and as many close confinements; nine separate maintenances, and two divorces. Nay, I have more than once traced her causing a *tête-à-tête* in the *Town and Country Magazine*, when the parties, perhaps, had never seen each other's face before in the course of their lives.

LADY SNEERWELL She certainly has talents, but her manner is gross.

This last is pure Beckett, an eighteenth-century equivalent of 'She had means, I fancy, though she lived like a pig.' And when we think of Arsene's flights of macabrely rational fancy, with their Congrevean mock-heroics – 'and the duster, whose burden up till now she had so bravely borne, fell from her fingers, to the dust, where having at once assumed the colour [grey] of its surroundings it disappeared until the following Spring' – or indeed Beckett's own, ruthlessly formalised so that geometry may impose some restraint on an otherwise uncontrolled variety of options, we see what Beckett has in common with predecessors such as Wilde and Sheridan, and all those in this tradition. We remember Lady Wishfort in Congreve's *Way of the World*:

Well, and how shall I receive him? In what figure shall I give his Heart the first Impression? There is a great deal in the first Impression. Shall I sit? – No, I won't sit – I'll walk – ay I'll walk from the Door upon his Entrance; and then turn full upon him – No, that will be too sudden. I'll lye – ay, I'll lye down – I'll receive him in my little Dressing-Room; there's a Couch – Yes, yes, I'll give the first Impression on a Couch – I won't lye neither, but loll and lean upon one Elbow; with one Foot a little dangling off, jogging in a thoughtful way – Yes – and then as soon as he appears, start, ay, start and be surpriz'd, and rise to meet him in a pretty Disorder – Yes – O nothing is more alluring than a Levee from a couch in some Confusion – It shews the Foot to advantage, and furnishes with Blushes, and re-composing Airs beyond Comparison. Hark! There's a Coach.

This is very close in mental process indeed to the great convolutions of self-examination that Beckett's 'heroes' in the dramas and the novels explore. What Beckett adds is the geometry. We think of Watt's way of advancing due east, or Molloy sucking the stones in his pockets turn and turn about, or Sam's

To think, when one is no longer young, when one is not yet old, that one is no longer young, that one is not yet old, that is perhaps something. To pause, towards the close of one's three hour day, and consider: the darkening ease, the brightening trouble; the pleasure pleasure because it was, the pain pain because it shall be; the glad acts grown proud, the proud acts grown stubborn; the panting the trembling towards a being gone, a being to come; and the true true no longer, and the false true not yet. And to decide not to smile after all, sitting in the shade, hearing the cicadas, wishing it were night, wishing it were morning, saying, No, it is not the heart, no it is not the liver, no, it is not the prostate, no, it is not the ovaries, no, it is muscular, it is nervous. Then the gnashing ends, or it goes on, and one is in the pit, in the hollow, the longing for longing gone, the horror of horror, and one is in the hollow, at the foot of all the hills at last, the ways down, the ways up, and free, free at last, for an instant free at last, nothing at last.

Even in the latest and most austere of the 'residual' novels the mannerism continues. 'Not count!' Mr Rooney exclaimed in the radio play of 1957 with yet another punning title, *All That Fall*: 'Not count! One of the few satisfactions in life!,' and the speaker in *Enough*, bent double in sympathy with her decayed companion whose 'trunk ran parallel with the ground' thinks over the possibilities of conversation:

Immediate continuous communication with immediate redeparture. Same thing with delayed redeparture. Delayed continuous communication with immediate redeptrure. Same thing with delayed redeparture. Immediate discontinuous communication with immediate redeparture. Same thing with delayed redeparture. Delayed discontinuous communication with immediate redeparture. Same thing with delayed redeparture.

But though Beckett has this in common with the Irish Comic Theatre, we should note a major difference. Sheridan's Maria says to Joseph Surface:

If to raise malicious smiles at the infirmities or misfortunes of those who have never injured us be the province of wit or humour, Heaven grant me a double portion of dullness!

Against this we must set the famous words from Beckett's *Watt*:

Where were we. The bitter, the hollow and – Haw! Haw! – the mirthless. The bitter laugh laughs at that which is not good, it is the ethical

laugh. The hollow laugh laughs at that which is not true, it is the intellectual laugh. Not good! Not true! Well well. But the mirthless laugh
is the dianoetic laugh, down the snout – Haw! – so. It is the laugh of
laughs, the *risus purus*, the laugh laughing at the laugh, the beholding,
the saluting of the highest joke, in a word the laugh that laughs – silence
please – at that which is unhappy.

In the end it is this that marks Beckett's theatre off from those other
dramatists in the tradition to which, on so many other counts, he
clearly belongs.

On the other hand it is important not to link him too closely with
those fellow-countrymen who may seem at first glance to be his obvious forbears in the Abbey Theatre. With the plays of Synge, in
spite of their humour and tramps, his art has no connection. Yeats's
tramps – not least in *The Cat and the Moon* and *Purgatory*, where
two are on an empty road, under a tree, waiting – resemble Gogo
and Didi in *Waiting For Godot* in their similar predicament (though
these are not specifically tramps). To one who is not Irish, the similar
idioms at times make the plays seem more closely related than they
are:

ESTRAGON You gave me a fright.
VLADIMIR I thought it was he.
ESTRAGON Who?
VLADIMIR Godot.
ESTRAGON Pah! The wind in the reeds.

We remember the title of Yeats's book. But there is really little connection. Beckett's preoccupations are different. As M. Arikha said to
me in a recent letter, 'The problem in Beckett is not the one of the
symbol but the one of the impact. *Godot* is not a presentation
of tramps, in fact they are *not* tramps, but a release of language in a

process of self-reduction.' He is surely correct. The most that can be claimed is that the form of the Noh play – which W. B. Yeats took from Pound's edition of Fenollosa's manuscript translations, best articulated by Yeats in classical form in that play on the theme of Cuchulain, Emer his wife, and Ethnie his mistress, *The Only Jealousy of Emer;* and in comedy in *The Cat and the Moon*; a structure built on opening lyric, followed by a stretch of narrative to a brief midway lyric, in its turn followed again by narrative, the whole rounded at the end by a lyric that bears some relation to the opening and central ones – is almost exactly the form of Beckett's *Play. Play* is, if you like, the sequel, set in purgatory, to any play on the eternal triangle. If one takes it further than that, Murphy's will regarding the disposal of his charred remains becomes apposite, and consideration of Beckett's debts to the Abbey Dramatists should

be burnt and placed in a paper bag and brought to the Abbey Theatre, Lr. Abbey Street, Dublin, and without pause into what the great and good Lord Chesterfield calls the necessary house, where their happiest hours have been spent ... and I desire that the claim be there pulled upon them, if possible during the performance of a piece, the whole to be executed without ceremony or show of grief.

Much closer to the central situation in *Waiting For Godot* is the great picture by W. B. Yeats's brother Jack, *The Two Travellers* (Tate Gallery), painted in 1942 when Beckett was living in hiding among the French farmers and peasants as a member of the resistance. This two-year experience of being 'on the run' seems to me by far the most important factor to bear in mind when discussing Beckett's post-war writings. The feeling is well captured as the *Texts For Nothing* open:

Suddenly, no, at last, long last, I couldn't any more, I couldn't go on

Someone said, You can't stay here. I couldn't stay there and I couldn't go on.

It left its indelible mark; and the great picture painted at this time by his close friend so much his senior, with its two figures perhaps about to part, perhaps only just having met, on an empty road that disappears in the direction of a barren mountain and sky, is closer to *Godot* than anything the artist's brother wrote.

Beckett's love of painting is indisputable. In the *Irish Times* in August 1945 he wrote of Jack Yeats:

He is with the great of our time, Kandinsky and Klee, Ballmer and Bram van Velde, Rouault and Braque, because he brings light, as only the great dare bring light, to the issueless predicament of existence, reduces the dark where there might have been, mathematically at least, a door.

Just before this he had carried a painting by Yeats in his possessions while working with the Red Cross on the front line. When Yeats exhibited in Paris in 1954, Beckett wrote:

What is incomparable in this great solitary achievement is its insistence upon returning to the most secret part of the mind which originates it and upon letting itself be lighted only by the day of the mind ...
Simply bow in wonder.[5]

But Jack Yeats was not the only painter who, with the van Veldes, won Beckett's close attention. The names of Kandinsky, Klee, and Braque mentioned in his review of Yeats were not chosen at random.

Braque had been introduced to Picasso by Apollinaire late in 1907, and in 1911, the year in which the friendship between the two painters was at its height, Picasso and Braque spent the summer together at Céret. These were the years in which they founded the cubist movement, and Braque was not only the first to show cubist works in public, but also probably painted the first cubist canvases. By the summer of 1911, the paintings in this manner of Picasso and Braque are virtally indistinguishable. The basic features are a linear grid, on which equal visual value is apportioned to both object and surroundings, the combination of several views of the object in a single image, and as a result a greater or lesser measure of abstraction.

In 1910 Robert Delaunay had become a member of the Cubist Group, only to move away soon after, like many others, to a more lyrical mode that Apollinaire dubbed 'Orphism'; a style that attempted to cultivate 'pure painting,' though obviously heavily indebted to and leaning on cubism. In 1911 Kandinsky invited Delaunay to exhibit with the artists of the *Blaue Reiter*. Klee came to Paris to see cubist works, and that autumn translated, as a result, some of Delaunay's notes on light for *Der Sturm*. Delaunay's 'Orphism' had taken to heart the austere lessons of analytic cubism, but substituted for its muted tones his own bright colours used in a more purely abstract way. For him, as for Jack Yeats, the principal elements were colour and light, and these were the elements that attracted both Klee and Kandinsky to him.

We can see perhaps the attraction that the formal clarity and use of light might have had for Beckett.[6] In *Come and Go* the three women, dressed in dull violet, dull red, and dull yellow, step in turn in and out of the stage's pool of light. An opening stage direction in *Play* reads :

Their speech is provoked by a spotlight projected on faces alone.

The transfer of light from one face to another is immediate. No blackout, i.e. return to almost complete darkness of opening, except where indicated.

The response to light is not quite immediate. At every solicitation a pause of about one second before utterance is achieved, except where a longer delay is indicated.

Indeed, as each of the three speaks directly ahead regardless of the other two in a toneless voice, and only when provoked, like three continuous straight lines of narration broken only by the cross-examination of the beam of light, and never overlapping; and as the order of solicitations may be reshuffled when the play is repeated, each fragment of each person's speech being self-contained and the over-all picture of the events described, though built up in an unfamiliar way, amounting to exactly the same once all have been completed, we are presented with an experience that may perhaps be called theatrical cubism, insofar as the emphasis is on muted colours, darkness and light, a mental and visual grid on which the fragments of the three monologues are constructed, and the skill with which the narrative shape of Act One is redistributed in Act Two with the same segments, is similar to cubist theory.

As for the value placed equally on objects and subjects, we remember among many such instances how Malone feels for the broken bowl of pipe he found:

Perhaps I thought it pretty, or felt for it that foul feeling of pity I have so often felt in the presence of things.

If Beckett learned to appreciate painting from long walks round Dublin Bay with Jack Yeats, he developed his interest well beyond that one Irishman's work, without ever losing his admiration for it.

Colour, a sharp sense of the emotive power of theatrical darkness and a pool of light on stage, rigid formality imposed on the flux of human living, and juxtaposing of hermetically sealed sentences having no contact with another person or voice on stage, but merely running in broken parallel to it, as in *Krapp's Last Tape,* all seem features better explained by comparison with the visual rather than the literary arts. But we must not forget that he is a dramatist, and the direction in which his dramas have increasingly progressed. Learning perhaps from Giacometti, whose work is somewhere between painting and drama, and who would work on a human form until ruthless pruning had reduced the life-size figure to one no bigger than a thumbnail, the direction of Beckett's later drama has been towards further and further austerity.

In his writings, we may trace the predicament of the unwilling will, the inarticulate voice, the croak in the mud, the hounded persona clarifying by careful negation his utterances, from the thirteen *Texts For Nothing* to the latest *Act Without Words*. It is only a short step from 'I'm a mere ventriloquist's dummy, I feel nothing, say nothing, he holds me in his arms and moves my lips ... all is dark, there is no one, what's the matter with my head, I must have left it in Ireland,'[7] to Beckett's full-scale novel *How It Is* :

in me that were without when the panting stops scraps of an ancient voice in me not mine

and the totally silent and crudely visual image of *Act Without Words II*, of a long pointed goad coming in from the wings of the stage and poking, hard, a sack from which a man emerges.

From whence comes the voice in *Eh Joe*? Who controls the goad? Who are the strangers who beat up Estragon before the play and during the interval? Who guards the guardians?

How are the intervals filled between these apparitions? Do my keepers snatch a little rest and sleep before setting about me afresh, how would that be? That would be very natural, to enable them to get back their strength. Do they play cards, the odd rubber, bowls, to recruit their spirits, are they entitled to a little recreation? I would say no, if I had a say, no recreation, just a short break, with something cold, even though they should not feel inclined, in the interests of their health. They like their work, I feel it in my bones![8]

Texts For Nothing is set in a first person *persona*, a solitary, who is speaking, if to anyone, to the reader, but certainly about himself. They all demonstrate a mind recording its feelings in a given context. To this extent they are dramatic monologues. Throughout them all we are reminded of the comment from the narrator of *From An Abandoned Work*:

No, there's no accounting for it, there's no accounting for anything, with a mind like the one I always had, always on the alert against itself ...

Throughout the *Texts For Nothing* we find the narrator's mind is continually 'on the alert against itself' – not to the point of silence, but often so that any word used has to be cancelled or withdrawn as soon as uttered. The first opens with the words 'Suddenly, no, at last, long last,' and we can see the narrator's refusal to use the dramatic word in place of the truthful one, the exact description of what happened. But how can anyone exactly describe what happened? This is the narrator's dilemma. The inclination towards truthful narration, and the impossibility of narrating the truth because one does not know what it is. 'Not good! Not true! Well well.' And so the narrator, after an attempt to describe his den. 'My den, I'll describe it, no, I can't' drags his body 'flat on my face in the dark earth' sustained by his own love for himself, which is a polite way of describing the instinct for self-preservation, until he has to sleep.

That's how I've held out till now. And this evening again it seems to be working, I'm in my arms, I'm holding myself in my arms, without much tenderness, but faithfully, faithfully. Sleep now, as under that ancient lamp, all twined together, tired out with so much talking, so much listening, so much toil and play.

So the denial of an ability to understand through big words –

I don't try to understand, I'll never try to understand any more, that's what you think, for the moment I'm here, always have been, always shall be, I won't be afraid of the big words any more, they are not big.

leads to the act of writing; the act of denial *is* the creative urge that sustains, be it toil or play, until sleep silences the conscious mind.

The mind 'always on the alert against itself,' rather like the contemporary heads of Picasso such as *Grande Tête* (linocut 1962) and *Tête De Femme* (linocut 1962) which comprise two interlocking profiles forming one over-all face staring out at the viewer, splits into two equal and opposite aspects as Beckett moves from *Texts For Nothing* to write plays.

In *Endgame* we are asked to remember 'the solitary child who turns himself into children, two, three, so as to be together, and whisper together, in the dark.' In other words, the pairs in the plays, Vladimir and Estragon, Pozzo and Lucky, Hamm and Clov, Nagg and Nell, Krapp old and young, Bolton and Holloway, Winnie and Willie, Man and his two women in *Play*, are double or opposite projections of an anterior solitary made to face each other. Instead of the *persona* speaking in his own person as in *Texts For Nothing*, two characters are created so they can face each other, and breed, in spite of being diametrically opposed; and what they breed is company. The solitary loneliness of farcical despair gives place to the burden of intolerable companionship. And with this, as we approach the later drama, we carry with us the picture of hopeless farce, rueful impotence, of being blessed in attaining to consciousness, but also damned in having only enough to realise that it is insufficient; as, for instance, in the first *Act Without Words* (1957).

In this mime a man is flung on stage and shown to be unable to cope with the incomprehensible forces that surround him. In the second *Act Without Words*, two men emerge in turn from their respective sacks, one to spend his stage life religiously, praying, taking pills, brooding, and spitting out his carrot; the other with intolerable enthusiasm, doing exercises, combing his hair, and continually consulting his watch. Each goes through his motions without being in the least aware that the other exists except as an object of heavy weight that must be carried.

In *Krapp's Last Tape*, Krapp is at least aware of his own recorded voice of years ago, though the tape cannot be aware of him.

Perhaps my best years are gone. [the tape ends] When there was a chance of happiness. But I wouldn't want them back. Not with the fire in me now. No, I wouldn't want them back.
Krapp motionless staring before him. The tape runs on in silence.

Would the present, much older Krapp, want them back? Little fire in him now. Sex has remained constant as a basis for pleasurable if transitory activity – but now his banana is kept locked in a drawer which he cannot always find; and when he does and eats it, he tosses the discarded skin into the pit with a vacuous stare.

With his white face and purple nose, this image of an old and weary man bathed in light listening to his tape-recorded youth seems, by the end, and especially in the final silence, like some Rembrandt portrait for a while come to life, now still. It is a moment of great theatrical poignance and power that can hold an audience silent for timeless minutes. Krapp, in common with some of the other narrators, has been able to prove to himself that he thinks, and therefore exists, by telling stories that he can listen to. Silence descends when he is more interested in listening to the stories than contributing his share. The uneasy partnership is broken when one refuses to play.

In *Happy Days*, Winnie has to take on herself three-quarters of the share. She is buried up to her waist in Act One, to her neck in Act Two, and her husband is uncommunicative.

Oh I know you were never one to talk, I worship you Winnie be mine and then nothing from that day forth only titbits from *Reynolds' News*.

When on a rare occasion Willie does vouchsafe an answer to the immense monologue of his wife it is brief and succinct :

What *is* a hog, Willie, please! *Pause.*

WILLIE Castrated male swine. (*Happy expression appears on Winnie's face.*) Reared for slaughter.

To which Winnie replies 'Oh this *is* a happy day!' and the climax of Act One is reached.

It is true that among many other things in her long and varied speech Winnie does quote a line from one of Yeats's Noh plays, *At The Hawk's Well*; a line, indeed, that Yeats had taken from the Japanese, together with his form: 'I call to the eye of the mind,' but again the resemblances are only superficial. Much more important is the fact that the old Beckettian preoccupations with time and personality are yet again annotated, even in the *clichés* of Winnie's gossip to herself:

I used to think ... (*pause*) ... I say I used to think there was no difference between one fraction of a second and the next. (*Pause.*) I used to say ... (*pause*) ... I say I used to say, Winnie, you the changeless, there is never any difference between one fraction of a second and the next. (*Pause.*) Why bring that up again? (*Pause.*) There is so little one can bring up, one brings up all ... Say no more. (*pause.*) But I must say more. (*Pause.*) Problem here.

She is imprisoned not only in the flesh, not only in the ground, but above all in her own limitations of thought, which even communication with another can only alleviate by the temporary distraction which we call for convenience 'happiness,' and thus a day in which it has been assumed to have been achieved, probably by violence or a violent image, a 'Happy Day.'

The narrators must talk, even when there is nothing to say, whether it is a text for nothing or on stage in front of an audience of an unattending husband. The goad continues to exist, even when the external manifestations of it are removed. The spotlight in *Play* solicits speech. Should the person on whom the light shines answer? They have no choice : What should they do?

Bite off my tongue and swallow it? Spit it out? Would that placate you? How the mind works still to be sure !

This is the real problem. Not whether one speaks one's thoughts or not, but the fact that one has them. To comprehend without the ability to be comprehensive, this is 'hellish half-light'; hence the ever-recurring longing for silence and the dark.

In *Words and Music* non-visual, radio, drama is stripped to its basic essentials : Words awakened from silence in a dark box, only to find itself cooped up with Music :

MUSIC *Small orchestra softly tuning up.*
WORDS Please! (*Tuning. Louder.*) Please! (*Tuning dies away.*) How much longer cooped up here in the dark? (*With loathing.*) With you!

and having been woken to tyrannical loathing by Music is made humble by a second voice designated Croak.

CROAK Joe.
WORDS (*humble*) My Lord.

With violent thumps of a club and a musical baton Croak tries to co-ordinate Music and Words. 'Age Music' is called for by a rap of the baton. The Age Music is soon interrupted by a violent thump of the club.

CROAK Together. (*Pause. Thump.*) Together! (*Pause. Violent thump.*) Together, dogs!

Finally Words tries to sing, and between thumps and sighs the Pozzo-Lucky, tyrant-slave routine is enacted in that little dark portable box we call a radio set. This shotgun partnership is completed with the climax of the song that Words and Music achieve, on the final word which is a euphemism for the female sexual organ. But the tyrant Croak, having brought this about, indeed compelled it, now is powerless. His club falls, and the sound of shuffling slippers dies away.

The themes of master and slave, sexual gratification, the problems of communication, of the solitary, of the probing mind turned inwards against itself in spite of itself by some compulsion, are all here, and at the same time Beckett has stripped the form of the radio play as he was later to strip television down to its basic individuality; a live head in a box brought into one's living room, at whose agonised changes of expression one may stare undeterred.

In *Imagination Dead Imagine*, the novel form is treated to the same ruthless stripping. If the imagination lives by imagining, then it should be able to imagine itself dead and thus find oblivion. But the problem is, as this little novel tells us in its title, that as the imagination imagines its own death it in fact imagines. It lives. Consciousness, then, is an intolerable curse, but the 'ordering' of consciousness, in both senses, is one of the less intolerable pastimes.

We come and we go, and we imagine past, present, and future, being able to guarantee none of them. Beckett's latest playlet or 'Dramaticule' is really a kind of ballet. The extraordinary compression his style has now achieved makes it possible to gather these themes together in bright focus, extending the range of his experiments in media, even as it shrinks the bones of his intellectual preoccupations. When it is all form and as little content as possible, then, as he wrote of James Joyce's final experiment, there will be neither prize nor penalty : 'Simply a series of stimulants to enable the kitten to catch its tail.'

Come and Go has three characters, who are female, but their ages are 'undeterminable' : Flo, dressed in dull yellow, Vi in dull red, and Ru in violet. They wear full-length coats, buttoned high, wear 'drab nondescript hats with enough brim to shade faces,' their hands are made up to be as visible as possible, and they speak 'as low as compatible with audibility.' Although they sit, it should not be clear what they are sitting on.

The three sit with their hands clasped in their laps, facing front, and there is a silence. Then Vi:

When did we three last meet?

A cross between an old girls' reunion and the witches in Macbeth.[9] She receives the answer from Ru 'Let us not speak.' Vi goes off and Flo turns to Ru:

FLO Ru.
RU Yes
FLO What do you think of Vi?

'I see little change,' Ru answers, and Flo moves to centre seat to whisper in Ru's ear. Appalled, Ru says 'Oh!' They look at each other, and Flo puts her finger to her lips, as Ru replies 'Does she not realise?' Flo answers 'God grant not,' and Vi returns and sits on the right.

After a silence Flo says 'Just sit together as we used to, in the playground at Miss Wade's.' And Ru answers 'On the log.'

With this 'Act One' ends, and after a silence Flo goes off left.

RU Vi.
VI Yes.
RU How do you find Flo?

'She seems much the same,' Vi answers, and the same ritual of whisper and appalled response takes place.

VI Oh! (Ru put her finger to her lips.) Has she not been told?

Ru answers 'God forbid,' and Flo returns to sit left.

After a silence Ru says 'Holding hands ... that way.' and Flo comments 'Dreaming of ... love.'

Then for Act Three it is Ru's turn to go out.

vi Flo.

FLO Yes.

vi How do you think Ru is looking?

FLO One sees little in this light. (*Vi moves to centre seat, whispers in Flo's ear. Appalled.*) Oh! (*They look at each other. Vi puts her finger to her lips.*) Does she not know?

and Vi answers 'Please God not.'

Ru comes back in and after a silence all three resume their front-facing pose. When they are still, Vi says

May we not speak of the old days? (*Silence*) Of what came after? (*Silence*) Shall we hold hands in the old way?

They do, in a cat's-cradle circle, still facing front, and Flo says 'I can feel the rings.' The stage direction tells us that there are no rings apparent.

This dramaticule is the very quintessence of the familiar Beckettian preoccupations. The same conversation is repeated three times. It is a three-act, pretty well a well-made play. Each gossips and is gossiped about in turn. Two of the others always think they know more about the third than the third does herself. They ask when they last met, but Ru, like Estragon, would rather not speak.

Ru is prepared to remember the log on which they used to sit at Miss Wade's – and indeed they may be on one now, we cannot tell. The past is forgotten, perhaps by emotional command. It is Vi who twice asks after the old days, but she is answered by silence. The past, it seems, they may not speak of. Perhaps it is unspeakable. The future of each is dreaded by her friends on her account. It holds a clear though unknown menace. Does the potential victim realise? Flo prays 'God grant not,' Ru says 'God forbid,' and Vi 'Please God not.' God is seen as one who confers benefits, one who forbids – perhaps it is he who has forbidden them to speak of the past; they are religious women.

And Vi mixes the random Irish colloquialism 'Please God not' with the penitent's prayer of desperation, 'PLEASE God *not*!' beautifully bringing into focus the two moods of the play: triviality of gossip about the past and friends' potential misfortunes, with the unanswered cry of anguish to a God who though unseen and absent must be placated. He can appear here no more than Godot can in *Godot*; but then, as in *Play*, Flo says 'One sees little in this light.' We see enough to know how little we can see. And together with a mandatory silence about the past, and proxy fears for the future, how do they spend the present? 'Dreaming of ... love.' So Krapp. So nearly all the later solitaries.

Childhood at Miss Wade's, adulthood dreaming of love, all fearing the future, each leaving alone, in turn. We remember the little, happy things of the past, Miss Wade's inconsequential log, dream about love in the present, and for the future, each of us must part with our company alone, and step out of the light of the intellect into the waiting darkness and silence, while others fear and are appalled about us. As we become aware of the future of our fellows we become horrified. Better not to have prescience. Better a limited knowledge of the future.

Perhaps that for which we grieve, our partial knowledge, should make us rejoice. So we laugh, down the snout – Haw! – so. And this *risus purus* springs from that split intellect, telling itself stories, even here where the burden of living is projected on to the immaculate and meticulous formality of Vi, Ru, and Flo; both horrified at and grateful for its limitations. We can merely pretend to ourselves that we feel the rings, pretend, even in the face of visible evidence, we are secure and happy; and meanwhile wait, hearing in the background the voices of courtesy, and encouragement, even praise:

They said to me, Come now, you're not a brute beast, think upon these things and you'll see how all becomes clear. And simple! They said to me, What skilled attention they get, all these dying of their wounds.[10]

Are those things that men adore and loathe/Their sole reality?
Sean McCutcheon as the Piper, Angela Fusco as the Singer,
Robert Derry as the Drummer

Notes

INTRODUCTION

1 W. B. Yeats, *Explorations* (London 1962), p. 156
2 James Joyce, *A Portrait of the Artist as a Young Man* (London 1964), pp. 204–5
3 In 1786 the Royal Irish Academy was founded and some time later the Scottish Highland Society, the Hiberno-Celtic Society, and the Gaelic Society. It was under the patronage of the Gaelic Society that the first complete edition and translation of an Irish legend was made : this was Theophilus O'Flanagan's edition of the Deirdre legend in 1808.
4 The work of Sylvester O'Halloran, Ferdinando Warner, J. H. Wynne, Charlotte Brooke, Joseph Cooper Walker, James Hely, Charles Vallancey, and a host of others can be attributed directly or indirectly to Macpherson's influence.
5 Edmund Curtis, *A History of Ireland* (London 1965), p. 330
6 Address of William Drennan at the opening of the institution, in Joseph Fisher and John Robb, *Royal Belfast Academical Institution Centenary Volume 1810–1910* (Belfast 1913), p. 205
7 Yeats, 'Under Ben Bulben,' *Collected Poems* (London 1961), pp. 398–9
8 Yeats, 'Easter 1916,' *Collected Poems*, p. 204
9 Lady Gregory, *Our Irish Theatre* (New York 1914), pp. 8–9
10 John Millington Synge, preface to *Poems and Translations* (Cuala 1909)
11 The quotations in the last part of this paragraph are from David Krause's essay, 'Sean O'Casey and the Higher Nationalism.'
12 Sean O'Casey, *Drums Under the Window* (London 1945), p. 266
13 See p. 133, David Krause, 'Sean O'Casey and the Higher Nationalism.'
14 F. X. Martin, '1916 – Myth, Fact, and Mystery,' *Studia Hibernica*, 7 (Dublin 1967 [1968]), pp. 10–11
15 Bernard Shaw, *The Matter with Ireland*, ed. David Greene and Dan Laurence (London 1962), p. 81
16 Shaw, *John Bull's Other Island* (London 1907), pp. xxiv, xxxv
17 Greene and Laurence, *The Matter with Ireland*, pp. 22–3
18 *Ibid.*
19 *Ibid.*, p. 252
20 *Ibid.*, p. 291

21 *Ibid.*, p. 279. See also Shaw, *John Bull's Other Island,* p. 23
22 Quoted in A. C. Ward, *George Bernard Shaw* (London 1966), p. 14. I have been unable to locate this reference in Shaw's works.
23 Greene and Laurence, *The Matter with Ireland,* p. 136
24 Yeats, 'Ego Dominus Tuus,' *Collected Poems,* p. 182

STARS OF THE ABBEY'S ASCENDANCY

1 J. W. Cunliffe, *English Literature in the Twentieth Century* (New York 1935), p. 109
2 *Joseph Holloway's Abbey Theatre,* ed. Robert Hogan and Michael J. O'Neill (Evanston, Ill. 1967), p. 113
3 Holloway, p. 172. See also Frank O'Connor, *My Father's Son* (London 1968), pp. 152, 191
4 David Greene and E. M. Stephens, *J. M. Synge* (New York 1959), pp. 229–30
5 Yeats to Frank O'Connor, quoted by Richard Ellmann in *Yeats: The Man and the Masks* (London 1961), p. 79
6 W. B. Yeats, *Autobiographies* (London 1955), p. 146
7 W. B. Yeats, *Essays and Introductions* (London 1961), p. 186
8 See *Autobiographies,* p. 141. Yeats and Shaw first met at the home of William Morris, early in 1888
9 Max Beerbohm, '1880,' *The Yellow Book,* January 1895, p. 278
10 Quoted by St John Ervine, in 'Portrait of W. B. Yeats,' *The Listener,* 1 Sept. 1955, p. 332
11 29 March 1894 to John O'Leary, quoted by Holloway, p. 106
12 Frank Hugh O'Donnell, *The Stage Irishman of the Pseudo-Celtic Drama* (London 1904), p. 9
13 *Letters of W. B. Yeats,* ed. Allan Wade (New York 1955), p. 466. The first paragraph of this letter, which is now in the Lilly Library, Indiana University, is omitted by Wade.
14 Foreword to *The Shaping of Modern Ireland,* ed. Conor Cruise O'Brien (London 1960), p. 1
15 See Oscar Wilde's *De Profundis, The Letters of Oscar Wilde,* ed. Rupert Hart-Davis (London 1962), p. 509
16 Letter to the *Daily Express,* 2 June 1892
17 Yeats, *A Vision* (London 1962), p. 35
18 *Letters to the New Island,* ed. Horace Reynolds (Cambridge, Mass. 1934), pp. 113–14
19 *Ibid.,* p. 134
20 Lady Gregory, *Our Irish Theatre* (London 1913), p. 103
21 *Autobiographies,* p. 121
22 See Ann Saddlemyer, 'The Heroic Discipline of the Looking-Glass,' *The World of W. B. Yeats,* ed. R. Skelton and A. Saddlemyer (Victoria 1965), pp. 96–101

23 In 1903, cf. 'The Poet and the Actor,' *Scattering Branches,* ed Stephen
     Gwynn (London 1940), pp. 133–4
24 *The Matter With Ireland,* ed. David H. Greene and Dan H. Laurence
     (London 1962), p. 81
25 *Ibid.,* p. 83
26 *Letters,* p. 279
27 Holloway, p. 6
28 Synge, *L'Européen,* 31 May 1902
29 James H. and M. E. Cousins, *We Two Together* (Madras 1950), p. 60 *passim*
30 *Ibid.,* 76
31 *Essays and Introductions,* p. 526
32 Holloway, p. 58

'INTELLECTUAL HATRED' AND 'INTELLECTUAL NATIONALISM': THE PARADOX OF PASSIONATE POLITICS

 1 *Letters to the New Island,* ed. Horace Reynolds (Cambridge, Mass. 1934),
     p. 6. Compare also pp. 103–4
 2 *The Letters of W. B. Yeats,* ed. Allan Wade (New York 1955), pp. 421–2
 3 W. B. Yeats, *Autobiographies* (London 1956), p. 355. (Hereafter cited in the
     text as A and followed by the page numbers.) When he looked back upon his
     experience as a political organiser, Yeats felt 'no different for it all, having but
     burgeoned and withered like a tree', p. 356.
 4 *The Variorum Editor of the Poems of W. B. Yeats,* ed. Peter Allt and
     Russell K. Alspach (New York 1957), p. 256. Hereafter cited in the text
     as V and followed by the page numbers.
 5 *Tribute to Thomas Davis* (Oxford 1947), p. 18. In the light of the ultimate
     division of Ireland, Yeats's next sentence is suggestive: 'How could we
     learn from the harsh Ulster nature ... a light that is the discovery of truth, or
     a sweetness that is obedience to its will?'
 6 Quoted by Edward Sheehy, 'Davis's Social Doctrines,' *Thomas Davis and
     Young Ireland,* ed. M. J. MacManus (Dublin 1945), p. 30. Hereafter cited
     as MacManus.
 7 *Ibid.,* p. 28
 8 T. F. O'Sullivan, *The Young Irelanders* (Tralee 1944), p. 44. Quoted from the
     prospectus for *The Nation* (15 October 1942). Hereafter cited as O'Sullivan.
 9 Quoted by Frank Gallagher, 'Davis and the Modern Revolution,' MacManus,
     p. 9
10 Quoted by Richard J. Loftus, *Nationalism in Modern Anglo-Irish Poetry*
     (Madison, Wisc. 1964), p. 6
11 Quoted by O'Sullivan, pp. 32 3
12 John Mitchel, *Jail Journal* (Dublin n.d.), p. 80
13 H. B. C. Pollard, *The Secret Societies of Ireland* (London 1922), p. 68. Not

confined to Mitchel, this remark is typical of Pollard's bitter denunciation of Ireland's 'malignant and terrible secret associations', p. x

14 Quoted by Kevin B. Nowlan, 'Charles Gavin Duffy and the Repeal Movement,' (O'Donnell Lecture, University College Dublin, May 1963), p. 19. This excellent article outlines the divisive issues clearly.

15 Quoted by O'Sullivan, p. 143. Compare Yeats's obvious enjoyment of 'the words of a medieval Gaelic poet, "We are a sword people and we go with the sword" ' (*Wheels and Butterflies,* London 1934), p. 13

16 *Prison Letters of Countess Markievicz,* ed. Esther Roper (London 1934), p. 226

17 Quoted by O'Sullivan, p. 131

18 *Ibid.,* p. 132

19 Quoted by Cathal O'Shannon, 'James Fintan Lalor,' MacManus, p. 70

20 *Ibid.,* p. 77. From Mitchel's short biography of Thomas Francis Meagher.

21 O'Sullivan, p. 80. At the same meeting Devin Reilly moved and Mitchel seconded a motion 'to inquire and report on the best and most effectual means of organising an armed National Guard', p. 80

22 Yeats, *Letters,* p. 39

23 Quoted by Sheehy, MacManus, p. 31

24 *A Servant of the Queen* (London 1938), p. 158. All quotations from Maud are from this book, cited hereafter by page references in the text.

25 'Discoveries: Second Series,' *Irish Renaissance,* ed. Robin Skelton and David R. Clark (Dublin 1965), p. 87

26 Of the many passages in *A Servant of the Queen* which illustrate Maud's delight in casting herself in the role of some mythical heroine, one is especially suggestive. According to Maud, Millevoye, her revolutionary friend whose 'whole ambition . . . was to win back Alsace-Lorraine for France,' urged her to an action she had no doubt already dreamed: 'Why don't you free Ireland as Joan of Arc freed France? You don't understand your own power. To hear a woman like you talk of going on the stage is infamous. Yes, you might become a great *actrice*; but if you became as great an *actrice* as Sarah Bernhardt, what of it? An *actrice* is only imitating other people's emotions; that is not living; that is only being a *cabotine,* nothing else. Have a more worthy ambition, free your own country, free Ireland', pp. 64–5. On still another occasion, at the Bal Irlandais in Paris, a 'florid gentleman . . . called for cheers for Ireland's Joan of Arc, which was responded to vociferously', p. 169. George Moore also records that 'Maud Gonne believes herself to be Joan of Arc' and suggests that Irish revolutionaries thought she 'would prove herself to be an Irish Joan of Arc', *Hail and Farewell,* 1, pp. 78, 91

27 Joseph Hone, *W. B. Yeats* (New York 1943), pp. 183–4

28 *Ibid.,* p. 223

29 Letter to Lady Gregory, in *Our Irish Theatre* (New York 1965), 211

30 *Irish Renaissance,* pp. 13–14

31 *Wheels and Butterflies,* p. 7

32 *Ibid.*, p. 5
33 *Ibid.*, p. 6
34 Quoted by Herbert Howarth, *The Irish Writers* 1880–1940 (London 1958), p. 294
35 The image of the imbedded bullet recalls Maud's pride in a brooch, which she 'always wore,' made from a bullet found in the grave of a French soldier 'who died for Ireland in 1798, p. 229
36 Quoted by John Unterecker, *A Reader's Guide to William Butler Yeats* (London 1959), pp. 120–1. Griffith was named in the diary but not in *Discoveries,* the published version.
37 Yeats omitted this poem, 'Reprisals,' from the *Collected Poems* because he feared Lady Gregory might be hurt by the implication that Robert was 'Among the other cheated dead.'
38 Yeats may have been thinking of himself and Maud in these wellknown lines : (v386)
   Did God in portioning wine and bread
   Give man His thought or His mere body?
39 W. B. Yeats, *Essays and Introductions* (London 1961), p. 249. 'Miss Maud Gonne could still gather great crowds,' Yeats wrote in 1907, '. . . and speak to them of "Mother Ireland with the crown of stars about her head"; but gradually the political movement she was associated with, finding it hard to build up any fine lasting thing, became content to attack little persons and little things. All movements are held together more by what they hate than by what they love, for love separates and individualises and quiets, but the nobler movements, the only movements on which literature can found itself, hate great and lasting things', pp. 249–50. Here apparently Yeats is not distinguishing between degrees or kinds of hatred, but between the qualities of its objects. The point is that he thought it necessary to distinguish between the hatred engendered by Maud's political movement and that of his movement, and he felt the force of both.
40 *Autobiographies* (London 1963), ii, p. 150. O'Casey also is talking indirectly about the two nationalistic groups. Recalling the riots over *The Plough and Stars,* he records : 'Sean felt a surge of hatred for Cathleen ni Houlihan sweeping over him. He saw now that the one who had the walk of a queen could be a bitch at times. She galled the hearts of her children who dared to be above the ordinary, and she often slew her best ones. She had hounded Parnell to death : she had yelled and torn at Yeats, at Synge, and now she was doing the same to him. What an old snarly gob she could be at times; an ignorant one too.'

TWO LECTURES ON THE IRISH THEATRE BY W. B. YEATS

1 See *Variorum Poems*, p. 851. See also *Letters*, p. 430

2 This play was written by Madeleine Lucette Ryley. Yeats saw it in Dublin in 1903 after its run of five hundred nights in London; whenever he attacked the commercial theatre it was his chief example. (See *Explorations*, pp. 112–13.)

3 These and subsequent marks of omission are in the original typescript.

4 This play was first produced in London on 21 February 1910.

5 Yeats has inserted in ink the phrase, 'to make his study of institutions', which replaces 'to create his victim' in the typescript.

6 Yeats has inserted in ink the phrase 'when they are bored,' which replaces 'to establish communication between them' in the typescript.

7 The word 'with' has been written in ink and replaces the phrase 'with mighty emotions and' in the typescript.

8 This word, like the one which concludes the following paragraph, is 'origin' in the typescript, but Yeats has added 'ality' in ink and so transformed it to 'originality.'

9 Yeats is referring, of course, to Raftery's poems about Mary Hynes. Lady Gregory had written about Raftery in her *Poets and Dreamers* in 1903 and Douglas Hyde had collected and edited his poems in the same year.

10 After 'St Patrick' there is a passage in the typescript which Yeats later deleted in ink: 'which is again typical of the people . . . they love their symbols and institutions, however, and so.'

11 In the typescript the sentence goes on 'and more of expressing feelings,' but Yeats has deleted this in ink and substituted 'emotionally' earlier in the sentence.

12 'Political' is in the typescript, but Yeats has deleted this and substituted 'poetical' in ink; it may have been difficult to distinguish between his pronunciation of the two words.

13 Yeats is, of course, referring to Synge, but he has not specified the sonnets he intended to read.

14 Yeats is referring to Giovanni Grasso, the principal actor and director of a group of players from Sicily who created a sensation in Europe and America in 1908 and 1909. Yeats had spoken about the group in a lecture on 'The Theatre' (7 March 1910): 'In the Sicilians you saw life leaping as a fountain. . . . All depended upon the joyous spontaneity of their art: they did the right thing because their instincts are right. . . . They had confidence in themselves; they poured themselves out; you felt they went home exhausted because they had expressed themselves so completely . . . the *heart* goes out in understanding of the Sicilians at every moment.' (The manuscript of this lecture is in the possession of Senator Yeats.)

15 That is, in London.

16 This does not make complete sense, but I have transcribed what is in the typescript.

17 'Politicians' is in the typescript, but Yeats has deleted this and substituted 'dramatists.'

18 A character in *Justice,* the play Yeats had referred to earlier in the lecture.

19 Yeats has deleted 'victor' in the typescript and substituted 'victim.'

20 An interesting slip for Yeats to make.

21 After 'propaganda' in the typescript there is 'of the' and a blank space, but Yeats later deleted 'of the.'

22 Yeats means, of course, 1896.

23 The first part of this sentence before Yeats altered it read as follows: 'The "Playboy" with its passionate love of mystery.'

24 Yeats, then, had also lectured at Mrs Fowler's on 18 December 1913. During the previous month, too, he had spoken at Mrs Fowler's for on 19 November 1913 he recorded in a manuscript diary: 'That day I . . . said at Mrs Fowler's: "I have thought for some time that I should be drawn into religious controversy by the natural development of things in Dublin. A mystical religious movement would be better than anticlericalism if the clericals attack us." ' (See A. N. Jeffares, *Yeats: Man and Poet* [London 1949], p. 320.)

25 Yeats has altered 'peace' in the typescript to 'happiness.'

26 In the printed text Yeats is identified as 'Member of the Senate of Dáil Éireann' and the following note is enclosed in square brackets: 'A man renowned in the world of letters, who, while justly placed amongst the foremost poets of our day, is no less a master of prose. We reverence a poet who strikes a chord of feeling in the Irish heart. For this inspired bard, fit recompense have we none, but such as we have, we give with grateful hearts.' – From the Latin Oration of the Public Orator (Sir Robert Tate) in the Classic Halls of Trinity College, Dublin, when conferring the Honorary Degree of Litt. D. upon Mr W. B. Yeats.

27 This phrase is 'one very prosaic fact' in the manuscript, and the sentence which follows it in the manuscript has been omitted from the printed text: 'No sooner did we begin our work in earnest than we found ourselves disliked and opposed by almost everybody.'

28 The last sentence is slightly different in the manuscript: 'In a few generations, and a few generations are but a short time in the history of a masterpiece, if you are a great artist or poet that crowd will speak of you with respect and in sufficient numbers study what you have made *most likely at some crisis of their lives* with pleasure and profit.' I have italicised the significant phrase which is not included in the printed text.

29 Yeats is referring to the *Memoir of the Great Original Zozimus* (Dublin 1871). Zozimus was the alias of Michael Moran (1794–1846).

30 Yeats first wrote 'fountain,' and even though the name is illegible in the manuscript he was thinking of a specific fountain.

31 The sentence which follows this sentence in the manuscript is omitted from the printed text: 'Yet when Miss O'Neill plays some part where she lacks the novelty and the protection of dialect, she has intonations and movements that one has seen before, that we are tired of, and her taste is not perfect.'

32 At this point Yeats has written and deleted in the manuscript 'and Goldsmith.'
33 I have followed the manuscript version of this phrase. The phrase is 'and which judge all by the light of some modern discovery' in the printed text, but the sense seems to demand 'moral,' not 'modern.'
34 This phrase is slightly different in the manuscript: 'without all the pleasant companionship in work and thought that belongs ... '
35 At the end of the manuscript Yeats has signed and dated the paper: 'W. B. Yeats/Nov. 1922.'

THE RISING

1 Emily Lawless, *Poems,* ed. P. Fallon (Dublin 1965), p. 13
2 Padraic Pearse, *Political Writings and Speeches* (Dublin, Cork, and Belfast 1924), p. 371
3 *Ibid.,* p. 336
4 *Dublin 1916,* ed. R. McHugh (London 1966), p. 48
5 'The Easter Week Executions' (1916), *The Matter with Ireland,* ed. David Greene and Dan Laurence (London 1962), p. 112
6 Ernie O'Malley, *On Another Man's Wound* (London 1936), pp. 43–6
7 Frank O'Connor, *An Only Child* (London 1961), pp. 154–6
8 Sean O'Faolain, *Vive Moi!* (London 1965), p. 105

YEATS, THEATRE, AND NATIONALISM

1 W. B. Yeats, *Essays and Introductions* (New York 1961), p. 526. In 1903 Yeats had written: 'I am a Nationalist, and certain of my intimate friends have made Irish politics the business of their lives, and this made certain thoughts habitual with me, and an accident made these thoughts take fire in such a way that I could give them dramatic expression. I had a very vivid dream one night, and I made *Cathleen ni Houlihan* out of this dream. But if some external necessity had forced me to write nothing but drama with an obviously patriotic intention, instead of letting my work shape itself under the casual impulses of dreams and daily thoughts, I would have lost, in a short time, the power to write movingly upon any theme. I could have aroused opinion; but I could not have touched the heart, for I would have been busy at the oakum-picking that is not the less mere journalism for being in dramatic form.' W. B. Yeats, *Explorations,* selected by Mrs W. B. Yeats (New York 1962), p. 116.
2 *Explorations,* p. 137
3 *Ibid.,* p. 152
4 *Ibid.,* p. 93
5 *Ibid.,* p. 103
6 *The Variorum Edition of the Poems of W. B. Yeats,* ed. Peter Allt and Russell K. Alspach (New York 1957), pp. 337–8

7 *Explorations*, p. 158. Cf. 'The Death of Synge': 'When a country produces a man of genius he never is what it wants or believes it wants; he is always unlike its idea of itself. In the eighteenth century Scotland believed itself religious, moral and gloomy, and its national poet Burns came not to speak of these things but to speak of lust and drink and drunken gaiety. Ireland, since the Young Irelanders, has given itself up to apologetics. Every impression of life or impulse of imagination has been examined to see if it helped or hurt the glory of Ireland or the political claim of Ireland. A sincere impression of life became at last impossible, all was apologetics. There was no longer an impartial imagination, delighting in whatever is naturally exciting. Synge was the rushing up of the buried fire, an explosion of all that had been denied or refused, a furious impartiality, an indifferent turbulent sorrow. His work, like that of Burns, was to say all the people did not want to have said. He was able to do this because Nature had made him incapable of a political idea.'
The Autobiography of William Butler Yeats (New York 1953), pp. 316–17

8 *Explorations*, p. 156

9 *Ibid.*, p. 120

10 *Ibid.*, pp. 109–10

11 *Ibid.*, p. 118

12 *Ibid.*, p. 72

13 *Ibid.*, pp. 146–7

14 Yeats, *Beltaine*, 2 (February 1900), p. 22. The passage continues: 'Dionysius, the Areopagite, wrote that "He has set the borders of the nations according to His angels." It is these angels, each one the genius of some race about to be unfolded, that are the founders of intellectual traditions; and as lovers understand in their first glance all that is to befall them, and as poets and musicians see the whole work in its first impulse, so races prophesy at their awakening whatever the generations that are to prolong their traditions shall accomplish in detail. It is only at the awakening – as in ancient Greece, or in Elizabethan England, or in contemporary Scandinavia – that great numbers of men understand that a right understanding of life and of destiny is more important than amusement. ... New races understand instinctively, because the future cries in their ears, that the old revelations are insufficient, and that all life is revelation beginning in miracle and enthusiasm, and dying out as it unfolds itself in what we have mistaken for progress. ... Progress is miracle, and it is sudden, because miracles are the work of an all-powerful energy, and nature in herself has no power except to die and to forget. If one studies one's own mind, one comes to think with Blake, that "every time less than a pulsation of the artery is equal to 6000 years, for in this period the poet's work is done; and all the great events of time start forth and are conceived in such a period, within a pulsation of the artery." ' Pp. 22-3.

15 *Explorations*, pp. 161, 153–4

16 *Ibid.*, p. 163

17 *Essays and Introductions,* p. 523
18 *Ibid.,* p. 102
19 *Explorations,* p. 154
20 *Ibid.,* p. 121
21 *Ibid.,* pp. 161–2
22 *Essays and Introductions,* p. 102
23 *Ibid.,* p. 103
24 *Ibid.,* p. 106
25 *Ibid.,* p. 103
26 *The Variorum Edition of the Plays of W. B. Yeats,* ed. Russell K. Alspach, assisted by Catharine C. Alspach (New York 1966), p. 704
27 *Essays and Introductions,* p. 107
28 *Ibid.,* pp. 104–5
29 *Variorum Poems,* p. 476
30 *Ibid.,* p. 565
31 *Letters on Poetry from W. B. Yeats to Dorothy Wellesley* (London, New York, Toronto 1940), p. 202
32 *Essays and Introductions,* p. 5
33 *Variorum Plays,* p. 453
34 *Essays and Introductions,* pp. 522–3
35 *Autobiography,* p. 286
36 *Essays and Introductions,* pp. 421–2
37 *Autobiography,* pp. 164–5. Cf. *A Vision* (New York 1938), pp. 141–5
38 *Ibid.,* p. 314
39 W. B. Yeats, *Mythologies* (New York 1959), p. 325
40 Cf. *Autobigraphy,* p. 314 and *Tribute to Thomas Davis* by W. B. Yeats (Oxford 1947), *passim*
41 *Autobiography,* pp. 286–7
42 *Essays and Introductions,* p. 525
43 *Ibid.,* p. 256
44 *Letters on Poetry,* p. 126
45 *Essays and Introductions,* pp. 313–14
46 *Variorum Poems,* pp. 391, 403, 565
47 *Letters on Poetry,* pp. 126–7
48 *Essays and Introductions,* p. 509
49 *Ibid.,* p. 523
50 *Ibid.,* pp. 513–14
51 *Ibid.,* p. 510
52 Leonard Nathan, *The Tragic Drama of William Butler Yeats: Figures in a Dance* (New York & London 1965), pp. 200–1. Natham quotes E. M. W. Tillyard, *Poetry Direct and Oblique* (London 1934), pp. 42–3
53 Helen Hennessy Vendler, *Yeats's Vision and the Later Plays* (Cambridge, Mass. 1963), p. 240

54 *Variorum Plays*, p. 1059

55 *Autobiography*, p. 286

56 *Variorum Plays*, p. 1060

57 *The Arrow*, pp. 1, 2 (24 November 1906). Quoted by S. B. Bushrui, *Yeats's Verse-Plays: The Revisions 1900–1910* (Oxford 1965), p. 2

58 *Essays and Introductions*, pp. 71–2

59 *Variorum Poems*, p. 585

60 Max Caulfield, *The Easter Rebellion* (New York, Chicago, San Francisco 1963), pp. 360, 369–70

61 Max Caulfield, *The Easter Rebellion* (London 1964), p. 133

62 *Variorum Plays*, pp. 399, 404

63 *Variorum Poems*, p. 374

64 Padraic Pearse, 'Ideal,' translated from the Irish by Thomas MacDonagh, *Poems of the Irish Revolutionary Brotherhood*, ed. Padraic Colum and Edward J. O'Brien (Boston 1916), pp. 24–5

65 *Variorum Poems*, p. 376

66 *Variorum Plays*, p. 229

67 *Explorations*, pp. 142–3

68   *The Letters of W. B. Yeats*, ed. Allan Wade (London 1954), p. 631

69 *Variorum Poems*, p. 405

70 *Ibid.*, p. 427

71 *Variorum Plays*, p. 766

72 *Ibid.*, p. 776

73 *Ibid.*, pp. 774–5

74 This thought is an extension of T. S. Eliot's remarks in *Selected Essays 1917–1932* (New York 1932), pp. 207–8

75 *Variorum Plays*, pp. 773–4.

76 *Explorations*, p. 109

77 W. B. Yeats, *On the Boiler* (Dublin n.d.), p. 31. Here he speaks of Shaw. In *Autobiography*, p. 317, he speaks of the 'furious impartiality' of Synge as the anti-self of the Irish temperament.

78 *Explorations*, p. 111

79 W. B. Yeats, *A Vision* (New York 1938), p. 25

80 *Essays and Introductions*, p. 339

81 *Autobiography*, p. 311

82 *Essays and Introductions*, p. 316

83 *Letters*, p. 654

84 *Ibid.*, p. 626

85 *Ibid.*, p. 654

86 Roger McHugh, 'Yeats and Irish Politics,' *Texas Quarterly*, v, 3 (Autumn 1962), p. 94

HIC AND ILLE: SHAW AND YEATS

1 From unpublished correspondence, Shaw to Yeats
2 *The Letters of W. B. Yeats,* ed. Allan Wade (London 1954), p. 59
3 The full texts of the letters from Yeats to Shaw referred to in this article are given below.
4 W. B. Yeats, *Autobiographies* (London 1956), pp. 134 and 283
5 *Florence Farr, Bernard Shaw, W. B. Yeats: Letters,* ed. Clifford Bax (London 1946), p. 16
6 *Ibid.,* p. ix and the preface to *Plays Pleasant, Complete Plays with Prefaces,* III (N.Y. 1963), p. 109
7 *Autobiographies,* p. 283
8 *Ibid.*
9 *Letters,* p. 335
10 *Complete Plays,* I, pp. 742, 743
11 *Ibid.,* II, p. 43
12 From an unpublished letter, W. G. Fay to W. B. Yeats
13 *Complete Plays,* II, p. 517
14 *Ibid.,* p. 605
15 *Ibid.,* p. 471
16 See *Bernard Shaw's Letters to Granville Barker,* ed. C. B. Purdom (London 1956), pp. 23 *et seq.*
17 *Letters,* p. 442
18 *Complete Plays,* II, p. 443
19 *Ibid.,* pp. 520, 521
20 Shaw's letter appeared in the *Irish Press* for 11 Feb. 1937. For Yeats's 'sexless' see *Letters,* p. 884.
21 W. B. Yeats, *A Vision* (London 1962), pp. 156-7

THE ABSENCE OF NATIONALISM IN THE WORK OF SAMUEL BECKETT

1 'Regatta Evening' by Jack Yeats
2 Beckett, *Texts for Nothing,* i
3 *The New Review,* II 5 (April 1932)
4 Quoted by Harold Hobson, 'Samuel Beckett, Dramatist of the Year,' *International Theatre Annual,* I (London 1956), and by Alan Schneider, 'Waiting for Beckett,' *Chelsea Review* (Autumn 1958).
5 'Hommage à Jack B. Yeats,' Les Lettres Nouvelles, 2e année (April 1954), pp. 619–20, trans. Dr Marilyn Rose
6 Cf. Beckett, *Murphy* (London 1938), pp. 111-12, 'There were three zones .. states of peace.'
7 *Texts for Nothing,* viii
8 *Ibid.,* vi
9 Cf. the homage to Hamlet's predicament in *Endgame:* 'If I don't kill that rat he'll die.'
10 *Endgame*